Dressage

Unscrambled

Bill Woods

Dressage

Unscrambled

Bill Woods

Half Halt Press, Inc.
Boonsboro, Maryland

Dressage Unscrambled

© 2009 Bill Woods

Published in the United States of America by
Half Halt Press, Inc.
P.O. Box 67
Boonsboro, MD 21713
www.halfhaltpress.com

Cover photograph by Bill Woods
Interior photographs by Bill Woods except where noted.
Illustrations by CW Woods
Original artwork for Gunnar illustrations on page 43 by
Don Nelson

Printed in the United States of America

Library of Congress Cataloging-in-Publication Data

Woods, Bill (William Close), 1948-
  Dressage unscrambled / Bill Woods.
     p. cm.
  ISBN 978-0-939481-82-8
  1. Dressage--Competitions--Anecdotes. 2. Dressage--Anecdotes. I. Title.
  SF309.6.W66 2009
  798.2'40207--dc22
                                        2009035281

For my parents,

Jean and Bill

Table of Contents

CENSORED RIDING

By The Man Who Mistook
His Life for Dressage

Bill Woods

1
Welcome to the Camp
(I Guess You All Know Why We're Here)

Minds work lots of different ways. Just ask Mesdames Myers and Briggs. Mine is intrinsically really organized—but I try very hard not to keep it that way. I'd bore myself silly. Hanging next to all my neat cerebral rows and columns, there's a big old garden rake that I use to stir myself up. With only a little effort (no caffeine required), I can get going like an old arcade game, complete with internal lights and sound effects.

Someone in a lesson says to me, "That was really good! Can you repeat that?" And I say, "Sorry, I wasn't listening. What was it about?"

A modicum of disorder is good for you, I believe. That's why these stories are arranged as they are.

I don't presume to be writing a dressage text, although if I did, I've always wanted to call a book *Dressage Answers Questioned*. More in the mode of Sally Swift, (they wouldn't let me use *Censored Riding*) with whom I rode back in the '80s, want to remind you of some images that can help you find your way through the morass of words that spill out of magazines and how-to books and threaten to drown us in pensive inactivity.

I also want to share some of the unlikely true stores that I've Gump-ishly witnessed over the years. If I pass along a few urban legends, it's accidental, but as has been said before, if they aren't true, they *should* be.

13

All this stuff has been floating around in my head for years. If I look different the next time you see me, it's because after getting this all on paper, I've been able to delete it from my mental hard drive, and all that empty space has allowed cranial subsidence and shrinkage to set in.

If you don't "get" any of the references in the text hereafter, remember, that's why God made Google. If that fails, e-mail me and I will elucidate.

With that, let us proceed into the Church of Dressage. Let the service begin...

2

Don't Know Much About History?
(How Important Horses Used to Be)

If you're much younger than I am (and pretty soon that's most everybody) and you aren't Amish, you aren't likely to think of horses in terms other than what your uncle bets on or as a pleasurable—maybe even passionate— diversion.

I'm just old enough to recall the milkwagon horse that delivered to my grandparents in West Philly. They lived in a row house that backed up on an alley and the rear of the houses on the next street. A good milk horse knew the route and could be sent with his wagon on down the street alone to wait at the end of the block while the milkman passed down the alley leaving a small order at each doorstep.

About the same time I remember horses pulling flatbeds that hauled the ashes from all the neighborhood coal furnaces down to a central location where they were rumored to be put on barges and dumped out at sea (ah, Naiveté!).

And when our pre-suburban house was being built in those early postwar years, a team of horses pulling a spreader dumped loads of cow manure on what we hoped would become a lawn someday.

People a little older than I can recall when horses in "real life" were the rule, not the exception. My mentor for many years, Major Anders Lindgren, recounts the times in his own experience when cavalry horses did the job of motorcycles, ATVs, and more. He tells one story when upon coming to a river, he commandeered a flatboat for his men, piled all their equipment onto it, and then had a group of the soldiers remount bareback and, holding onto the gunwales of the boat, swim the horses across while pulling the boat along, keeping their cargo safe and dry.

Of course, before the inventions of the steam engine and later the internal combustion engine, other than wind and water power (and an occasional ox), the horse was for centuries the world's prime extra-human motive power, not only to transport people and goods everywhere they needed to go, but also to provide stationary power to mill grain, raise water, power sawmills and paper mills, drill for oil, power lifts and cranes, turn paddle wheels on ferry boats, and perform a thousand other tasks.

Out of curiosity I did some research to see how many horses are alive on the planet in 2008. Can you guess? According to the Food and Agriculture Organization of the United Nations, the global horse population is about 60 million. The U.S. alone has 9.5 million, by far more than any other country. The same source reports that nine other countries have horse populations of more than a million. They are:

China	7.4 million
Mexico	6.2 million
Brazil	5.7 million
Argentina	3.6 million
Colombia	2.5 million
Mongolia	2.0 million
Ethiopia	1.6 million
Russian Federation	1.3 million
Kazakhstan	1.2 million

Guam (20) and Grenada (30) had the lowest totals. Two countries, Rwanda and St. Helena, reported having no horses. Don't let anybody sell you a riding vacation there!

The report reveals that back in 1915, the U.S. equine population reached its all time peak: 21 million. Mechanization on the farms and people moving to the cities reduced that total drastically to a low of approximately 2 million in the early 1950s. Our post war economic boom and the increase in leisure time have helped that number re-grow since then.

Currently, the nearly 60 million horses in the world are split among the continents like this: 7.2 million horses in Europe, 12 million in North America, 10.5 million in Asia/Pacific Rim and 15 million in South America.

Thanks to the internet, I also uncovered these facts that you should commit to memory: The total size of the national livestock herd of Mongolia is 33 million, including 15.1 million sheep, 11 million goats, 3.8 million, cattle, 3.1 million horses (including ponies, mules, and donkeys), *and 350,000 amels.*

Still thirsting for knowledge? Drink in these Mongolian camel factoids, and you'll never lack fodder for cocktail party conversation:

"The two-humped bactrian camel is one of the world's rarest and most unique camels known to man. Besides Mongolia, this camel is also popular in Russia and China. The Mongolian camel population is estimated at 355,600, which is believed to be about 1.8 per cent of the world's camels. Although the camel is a domesticated animal of herders, in relation to the other domesticated herder livestock, the camels are by far the more durable and better adapted to Mongolia's harsh wintry weather. Its wool coat, which is shed in the summer, acts as an insulator in the winter. An adult male camel can give up to 18 kilograms of wool per year. A female camel can impressively produce up to 575 liters of milk during her 18 month lactation period. A camel's health can also be determined by the state of their humps, which will

droop or sag when ill or thirsty. A camel typically drinks 40-50 liters of water a day. One that has not drunk for several days can consume nearly 200 liters in a single day." (See mongolia-resorts.com)

Getting back to horses, I was overwhelmed by the use (and loss) of horses during the World Wars of the last century. In WW II, according to the U.S. National Agricultural Statistics Service, the German Army employed more than one million horses—more horses, in fact, than they had tanks.

Jilly Cooper in *Animals in War* writes "Eight million [horses] died in the Great War [that's WW I] alone, most from exposure, disease and starvation." I have read elsewhere that the equine death toll in Europe in WW II exceeded another seven million. These are depressing and astonishing numbers.

I also discovered the following equally elucidating but somewhat more cheerful facts:

In the U.S. in the mid-1880s, before steam and electrical propulsion took over completely, there were 100,000 horses and mules pulling 18,000 horse cars on 3,500 miles of track.

In 1900, records show the horse population *in U.S. cities* exceeding 3.5 million. And lastly, this tidbit: in Chicago at the turn of that century 82,000 horses were producing 600,000 tons of manure per year.

When you have horses, isn't THAT what it always comes down to?

3

The "Helps"
De-jargonize and See the Light

Back in the early '90s, my wife, Susan, was conducting an instructor workshop for the USDF. The format included discussion and critique of assigned lessons taught by the participating instructors to "guinea pig" demo riders. One of the participants was from the Netherlands and knew a lot about riding and teaching. However, her only English was the kind she'd learned in high school, and it didn't include any formal riding terminology. So to be able to function in the States as a dressage instructor, she was taking the workshop to improve her language skills.

At one point during her assigned lesson, at a loss for the word "aids," she substituted "the helps."

I particularly liked this term because so often we get immersed in the technical terminology—the jargon—and forget just what the term in its stripped-down, raw form means to convey. Thinking of "the aids" for a turn, for instance, can devolve into a formulaic recitation of a memorized recipe. The "helps" is really much more what the aids are all about—giving the horse the information he needs at that moment to be balanced or realigned or whatever kind of help he needs to perform the movement you desire. Try thinking of "the helps" to make your input to your horse more personalized and appropriate to the situation than a more generic use of "the aids" can provide.

4
Speaking of Recipes....
(and the Queens)

Along the lines of "the aids" as "helps," let me go way back to the beginning of the riding experience. When I used to teach beginners years ago, students would always want to know the recipe to make each movement or figure. Then it was for a circle; now it's for a shoulder-in or a turn on the haunches.

I always told them that while it was OK to learn the recipes, the Betty Crocker method of riding has some conceptual limitations. Instead, I always think of a "Template Model" to visualize how to make things happen.

Way back in Junior High School I had to take a semester of Metal Shop. Our assigned semester project was to make a candlestick holder, the base of which was an upright bar of soft iron that we had to bend into an elaborate S-shaped scroll. To make the curves accurate, we had a full sized pattern—a template—drawn out on graph paper. We would over and over put the iron bar in a jig, make a small bend, and then lay the bar over the template to see if each part of our curve matched the drawn one.

This idea demonstrates a way to look at guiding and shaping your horse. To ride a circle, for example, it wouldn't be wrong to say the recipe includes *sitting with your inside seatbone forward, putting your inner leg at the girth and your outside one back, positioning the horse to the inside and suppling his inside jaw with your inner rein, and supporting his outside shoulder with your outer rein.*

The recipe works just fine in an ideal world. But let me describe a less-than-ideal (though slightly exaggerated) scenario that reveals the recipe's shortcoming.

Your horse is trotting on the 20-meter circle with your aids applied according to the recipe above. But to make life more interesting, just outside the eastern edge of its circumference we dump a huge pile of oats and just beyond its western edge we wheel in a circus wagon holding three fearsome tigers. Now the recipe doesn't work so well. On the eastern side your horse wants to overbend in and bulge his outside shoulder radically towards the oats. On the western side he wants to counterflex and shy violently inward away from the cats.

So going back to the template model, first you must visualize the problem from above. Picture the line over the ground of the 20-meter circle you're trying to navigate. Then adjust your aids to make the horse's body conform to that arc as you travel around it. You can probably imagine that on the east side, your inner leg will hardly have to do anything but your outside leg and outside rein will dominate as they build a wall to keep him from leaning towards the oats. On the opposite side of the circle those aids won't do you any good at all. They'll only make him fall in off the track further. There you'll need to massively reinforce the inner leg/inner rein to keep him bent and to yield him back over into the outside rein and onto the line you mean to follow. So in this example the aids your horse needs to feel on one half of each circle will be almost completely opposite from what he needs on the other half. That's why the template and not the recipe.

Let's stay with the template idea a little longer so I can talk about ocean liners. Even now from time to time in a clinic I'll ask the riders for something like a turn on the haunches and a few will look a little puzzled and say to me, "What are the aids for that?"

My first question in return is "Do you know what one looks like?" I ask them to describe the template—what the movement looks like if you were hanging in the rafters watching it from above.

Then I tell them about being taken to New York City when I was very young. Back then (we're talking 1950s) we lived near Philadelphia, and a big

19

treat was going over to New York on a Wednesday because that was the day the big transatlantic liners arrived from Europe, churned into the harbor amid sirens and fountains from the fireboats, and docked at their berths along the Hudson River. In those days the liners (not the *QE2* then but the original *Queen Mary* and *Queen Elizabeth* and *S.S. United States*) didn't have bow thrusters and lateral props to help them maneuver into their piers. Instead, each docking was attended to by half a dozen tugboats.

The captain stationed himself on the wing of the bridge with a megaphone where he could view *his* template of what needed to be done, and he would shout down to each tug in turn as to what part of his ship they should push or pull into place.

With that image in mind I propose to my students (Remember the ones still trying to figure out the turn on the haunches?) that if they can picture the template they need and if the horse is responsive to their leg and hand,

they should be able to "invent" the aids they need to produce the right result. Whether it's a turn on the haunches or a leg yield on the diagonal or a shoulder in up the centerline, they're the captain and their legs are the "tugboats" that are placed and activated as needed to shepherd the horse through the movement.

Learning the aids this way gets riders out of the prison of their left brain and helps them better to feel their way through movements and how those "helps" start to shape, balance, and connect their horse.

5
Random Judging Tales
(to make you feel better)

No matter how experienced a rider is, he or she had to start someplace. If showing is new to you, or terrifying, you are hardly the first person ever to have felt that emotion. Likewise, nowadays every judge has to have gone through that same learning-from-the-bottom-up experience. Not only have they probably seen most everything before from the judge's booth, but they've also seen and felt it from your side of C.

Be reassured that any judge worthy of the title ought to be able to empathize with you and is probably pulling for you to figure things out, get them right, and succeed.

So here are a handful of stories—all 100 percent true—that I can recount firsthand to indicate that we're all (or have been) in the same boat.

Judging Story #1
(In case you think you're the only person ever to get nervous)

I was judging a schooling show years ago at a little place in Massachusetts when a novicey middle-aged lady came down the centerline to begin her test. She halted at X, saluted rather smartly, and proceeded towards me. As she came closer and closer, rather than setting her horse up for the turn, she let her horse trickle to a stop with his chin hanging over C, protruding into my trailer. Then leaning forward with her eyes as big and blank as the front of a

21

greyhound bus, she croaked in a barely audible whisper, "I've never done this before, and I can't remember *anything!*"

Needless to say, I tried to assuage her fears, invited her to consider trying to breathe, and helped direct her on her way.

Judging Story #2
(For people who get a little ahead of themselves)

An old version of Training Test 3 some years ago called for the rider to make a downward transition to trot coming up the long side of the arena towards the judge, then pass by the booth from M to C to H, cross the diagonal, turn onto the centerline at A, and finish with the salute at X.

In one test the rider made her canter to trot correctly but got a little ahead of herself and turned onto the centerline going *away* from me. I knew immediately she was off course, but curiosity got the best of me, and I had to see what she'd do next. Naturally (or not), she halted, made her salute, and then noticed she was facing the exit instead of the judge. After she peered over her shoulder rather sheepishly and offered a tentative little wave, I suggested she might go back to M and ride that last short side, diagonal, and centerline towards me rather than away.

Judging Story #3
(If you're self-conscious about riding all alone)

I was judging another schooling show and rang the bell as an acquaintance (who happened to be another judge) rode by my booth preparing for her test. As she came down the centerline and halted, I noticed a small pony with a blue-jeansed rider had halted on the centerline immediately behind her.

"Uh, who's your friend?" I called.

The competitor looked quite perplexed till I suggested, "Look behind you," at which point she was more shocked and amazed than I was. But very quick on the uptake, she said to the little girl, "Here, follow me," and escorted her on a trip once around the arena before ushering her out the gate and sending her on her way.

Later, the ring steward reported that our visitor was a neighborhood child from down the road who was on a Saturday morning trail ride with her pony when she saw the horse show and, before anyone could catch her, figured she should join in.

Judging Story #4
(Should you believe that judges themselves don't get mortified too)

I had first judged a little backyard show in 1970, been to my first judge's forum in 1972, taken a learner judge's course in '76, and gone through the formal procedure of doing the then yearlong small "r" course to get my license in 1982.

Finally in June of 1983, I was about to officiate at my first AHSA-recognized competition, and it wasn't a little one. There I was at C in Arena 4 of the six ring New England Dressage Association Summer Show and feeling quite nervous, self conscious, and painfully determined to get every number and comment exactly right.

I had just blown my whistle and my first ever competitor was on her way down the centerline towards me when, like a nightmarish apparition, my new (by less than a month) father-in-law popped up in front of me, totally blocking out my view of the rider, so that he could take a photo of me in my judge's booth.

I'm sorry to admit that he, the rider, and anyone within 100 yards heard a rather strident admonition from me in language that doesn't usually accompany the salute at X!

6
Vending Machines

I must have been traveling too often, staying in too many hotels....

You know how down by the ice machine next to the elevators they always have vending machines? The ones with a big Plexiglas window and a whole mess of snack items—Sun Chips and Fritos and Ring Dings and Lorna

Doones—each stacked on copper spiral holders all in rows and columns? And you put your 75 or 85 cents in the slot, the machine blinks READY READY READY, and all you have to do is "Select." Punch B-4 and grind grind fwoop, out the slot at the bottom comes your Snickers. E-6 and fwoop, here are the Cheetos. In other words, once you've made the preparation, the machine is equally, universally prepared to deliver you anything on its menu.

It strikes me that it isn't a bad idea to think of making your horse a bit like one of those vending machines. This is what I mean:

It drives me a little batty when someone has been trotting around for five minutes; I ask them to make a transition to halt; and they say, "Wait, I have to prepare him." Or if they've made six halt-trots: I ask them to canter, and they give me the "wait a minute" response. Or after six leg yieldings they have to get the horse ready for a turn on the haunches.

Do I mean you shouldn't prepare for those things? It's not that at all. But like the vending machine that, once prepared, is able to deliver you *anything*, so should your horse (if he's on the aids) be equally ready to offer you whatever movement you need next with no more than the appropriate positioning and a rebalancing half halt or two.

"Preparation" should be universal. Ready for one thing is supposed to be ready for all things.

An underlying theme within the subtlety of riding a dressage horse is keeping up a fairly constant nonverbal conversational stream of "If I wanted to, could I _____?" with him. In the beginning, the questions are blatant, broad strokes: Ask him to make a transition… Did it work? From his responses trial by trial, you learn to file away in your memory what he needed to feel like in advance for that transition to have worked when and how you wanted it to.

Tuning in to how a horse has to feel before the fact brings you to where, like lawyers in those courtroom novels, you never really ask an overt question without knowing what the answer is going to be. Asking for a downward transition and finding it's not there becomes an "oops moment." We try to avoid those!

An old rulebook definition of a half halt described it in terms of creating or re-creating attention and balance. If he's upright, holding himself, alignable, and listening to you, any movement ought to be there for you. And by maintaining the intimate interaction with him that queries "Could I…," you encourage and enforce the balance and attention required to make all things universally and equally available.

Like the vending machine.

7

Contact

Former USET dressage coach Bengt Ljungquist described the feeling of the horse taking the contact with the bit as follows: Imagine you're standing on top of an arched footbridge over a gently flowing stream. In your hand you hold a block of wood and tied to the block is a long string. Holding the loose end of the string you drop the block over the railing and into the water.

The soft, consistent pressure that the stream exerts on the block and transfers up through the string into your elastic elbows is like the feeling of the horse accepting contact and reaching into your hand.

Another one: You know those old fashioned Wurlitzer juke boxes that you find in retro style bars and restaurants? The kind that have the concentric rings of transparent, liquid-filled tubes that arc around the sides and top, change colors, and have the bubbles that flow through them?

Well, imagine your reins are like those hollow tubes with the bubbles. When the horse is correctly on the aids, you're making the bubbles flow from your hand towards the bit. If the bubbles are stationary in the tubes or flowing from the bit back toward your hands, then, despite your horse being flexed at the poll, he's not on the bit but most likely backed off, posing, hiding behind the leg, and not filling the reins with

26

correct contact. If, on the other hand, those bubbles are gushing out the tubes like a torrent through a firehose, you've got a different problem!

Another difficulty with contact involves riders who have weight in the reins, but rigidity in their forearms or wrists keeps the horse from connecting through his topline from hindquarters to the bit.

A long time ago someone impressed upon me that your elbows and forearms "belong to the horse" and are like a continuation of the reins. To keep from blocking the connection with stiff wrists or "Popeye arms," imagine that your forearms are like hollow pipes and the reins, though held in your hands, pass up through those pipes and hook directly into the back of your elbows without suffering from resistance in between.

It often strikes me that many riders have trouble establishing the feel of a "following hand." This concept doesn't equate directly to the messages imparted through your reins, but rather with the open line on your phone or the carrier wave on your radio that remains steady until modulated when you want to send information over it.

In an old British Horse Society manual on stable management I once saw a diagram on how to arrange the tie in a standing stall (as opposed to a box stall) so that the horse wouldn't put his foot over a too-long rope but so that he could still lie down if he wanted. The tie rope was connected to his halter, but instead of fastening directly to the wall in front of him, it passed through a metal ring attached to the wall and then hung vertically with a wooden block weighted on its free end. If the horse backed up or lay down, he (within limits) pulled the weight up but the block kept any slack from developing. If he stepped forward, the rope remained gently taut because the weight pulled the rope farther through the ring.

Riders looking to establish the elastic following hand that goes with the horse's mouth might imagine a similar rope hooked to the back of their elbow and threaded over a pulley behind their arm. If the horse's head raises or comes back, the wooden block automatically absorbs the potential slack in the rein. If the horse's head comes down or forward, the hands sympathetically follow but the weighted rope on the pulley allows the same contact to be maintained.

I should mention that if the rider doesn't want the head going forward or down, the following hand is interrupted by a momentarily braced back supported by the legs and a non-allowing hand that conveys to the horse what boundaries are not to be overstepped.

8

Self-Carriage
(Angels and Demons Redux)

I try to stay up to date on the literature of our sport. One of my favorite 20th century dressage authors is Eldridge Cleaver, whom you may remember, wrote **Soul on Ice** as a Black Panther back in the '60s. His contribution to my dressage lexicon was "If you aren't part of the solution, you're part of the problem," a reminder that horses never stay the same. That one way or the other, we are "training" them, even if the message we're delivering is something like "It's OK to fall asleep," or "Please ignore my half halt."

Another dressage text in the bookstores is by Dan Brown who authored **The Da Vinci Code**. It's called **Angels and Demons** and, ostensibly, it's about intrigue and malfeasance within rogue elements at the Vatican. The plot hinges on the super secret work of a Swiss hi-tech firm that has devised a way to harness the much coveted powers of controlled nuclear fusion.

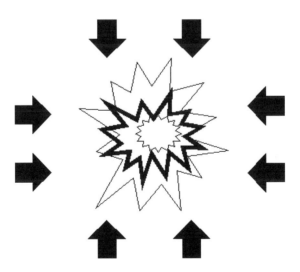

As Brown explains, the process of controlled fusion involves extremely hot plasma gases—like the center of our sun—on the order of 50 million degrees. A major sticking point in its development is that the gases are so hot that they would simply burn through and vaporize any vessel in which you'd try to contain them. But the plasma is ionized, that is, it carries an electrical charge; so the bad guys are able to construct a "magnetic bottle," essentially a force field that suspends the hot gases in space. Electromagnets surround the plasma and act on it equally on all sides so that it never comes in physical contact with what holds it in place.

Admittedly the analogy isn't quite perfect, but Brown is clearly describing a horse in self-carriage. In real life you do bring the sides of your "bottle" into contact with the horse when you make a half halt, and likewise, you may maintain a light, enveloping leg and a soft receiving hand. But the idea of the horse sustaining his "uprightness," his lateral and longitudinal balance, based upon your intermittent inputs that tell him how to hold himself rather than a crutch-like physical presence is valid. Think of your half halts as re-centering him in the "bottle" before he ever gets so close to the walls as to be able to burn through them.

9

More Show Stories
(What is "Unauthorized Assistance"?)

At a Pony Club Dressage Rally I was judging a class of D-1s riding Training Test 1 in a rather lush grass arena when the plump Thelwell entry rounded the corner, drifted off the track, stopped, dropped its head, and began to graze. Had I not climbed out of my booth and hauled his head up, that pony would most likely still be there!

This story was easily topped by Gisela Holstein, the FEI judge from Ireland, who tells the story of judging at a big horse trials in England, again on grass, where the arenas were set on the lawn in front of a stately castle. Early in the morning the grass was slippery from a heavy dew, and a caulkless horse in an adjacent arena lost his footing and slid onto his side in front of his judge.

To complicate matters, as he lay there, the horse discovered the "salad bar" inches from his muzzle, and began grazing placidly out the side of his mouth. Despite his rider's urgings, the horse showed no interest in getting up at which point the judge called plaintively to Gisela, "What do I do now?"

Her reply: "Well, you better go out there and start kicking him too, or we'll never get done by lunchtime!"

Then there's S judge Renate Ruzich's story of a trainer who had secured permission from show management to read his student's dressage test to him in German instead of English—perfectly legal. Legal until Renate, a native German speaker, noticed that he wasn't just reading the words on the test sheet but was, in German, adding quite a few helpful but totally illegal hints about how to ride through the movements.

As Renate tells it, he was quite sure he'd pulled a fast one, until at the test's conclusion, Renate called him up to the booth and asked him *in German* just what he thought he was doing!

And one more: I was judging an Arabian Dressage show out in the Midwest and during one particularly inept amateur Training Level test, it became apparent that the reader was saying more to the rider than just the next movement each time she went by. Sorry, folks, but you just *can't* do that. So I blew my whistle, put the test on pause, and invited the reader to come talk things over.

"No coaching allowed," I explained.

"But I wasn't coaching," she said. "I was just telling her not to cry."

10

Why Complain If You Can Just Shake Your Head?
Judging Foibles

When you've been around the show world for a while, you know not to take any given score you get too seriously. Yes, judging standards have improved immeasurably since "the old days." Beginning in the mid '70s, increasingly elaborate and comprehensive educational programs for judges and judge wannabes have eliminated many of the oddest and most egregious examples of judges' flights of fancy. Most of the time we can hope that "a 7 is a 7 is a 7" no matter whom you find yourself riding in front of.

Even so, there will be exceptions—an unrealistically high appraisal of your horse's performance one day and an especially stingy one another day. Consequently, although I want my students to look over their tests and see what kind of useful feedback they can glean, I remind them not to be too euphoric or too suicidal over any particular test result. If, on the other hand, a bunch of judges in a row all tell them the same thing, THAT'S worth taking serious note of!

So with those provisos in mind, it's time for an anecdote from a recent show. The victim in this tale we'll call "Bernice" in order to preserve her anonymity. She rides a highly-trained, older schoolmaster whose knowledge extends well beyond the level where she's working. Bernice showed this horse in the same test—Third Level Test 3—each day, both Saturday and Sunday. On Saturday she had a very pleasant and more than workmanlike ride. It had its brighter and less bright spots but, as a sophisticated and neutral observer told me, Bernice was sitting much better than in the past, had her horse in front of the leg, and was "looking like a dressage rider." His medium and extended trots weren't a highlight and she didn't ask enough in his canter, but she had clean changes and the general impression was pretty nice. I figured "a few too many 5s" and gave it a 58 percent in my head. Saturday's judge didn't quite agree and gave it a 55 percent that I thought was a bit low, but hey, so it goes.

On Sunday Bernice rode the same test in front of a different judge in a different arena. She had a fruitful and effective warm-up, but right before the test decided to remove her brand new top hat's rain cover ... at which point I noticed the bow was in the front and she had her hat on BACKWARDS. Of course, in getting it fixed, she irreparably loosened that thing that dressage women use to hold their hair in place such that it began to come unstuck and remove itself and flutter around over her shoulder as the test progressed.

The ride began well, but at the start of the first trot half pass (the one to the left from B to G), her horse began to flip his head rather wildly and proceeded to continue flipping it during the extended trot, the halt/rein-back, and the left shoulder-in. It had become clear to me that his tongue was over the bit and he couldn't get it back.

So in the middle of the shoulder-in, Bernice stopped dead to let him fix it. She resumed, but the scores she had just earned should have been a string of 3s or 4s and something like a 1 for her unauthorized pause.

All this got her so befuddled that instead of riding the S turn from B to X to E and a right half pass, she made a FULL 10-meter circle at B and another left half pass like the one she'd done four movements earlier (though to give them *some* credit, at least this time he didn't toss his head).

Then total confusion ensued because the judge didn't notice she was off course and ring the bell. Bernice, no dumb cookie despite her increasingly eccentric appearance by this point, stopped when she got to C, and said "I've made a mistake." The judge first told her, "No, everything is OK. Keep going." Then when she realized that something was indeed seriously amiss, the judge failed again to ring the bell, stop the rider, and send her back to where the error of course began. So Bernice soldiered on with the turns on the haunches and the canter work having never gone back to execute the missing movements.

By rights, there should have been two zeros in a row along with the error of course, but wouldn't you know it, when she got her test back, she'd scored 2 percent *higher* than she had with her nice test the day before. Including a 6 for a movement she didn't do at all.

I, as a judge, can make no apologies for this, just an example of random wackiness that demonstrates human fallibility on all parts and hopes to be the exception, not the rule. Bernice remains of good cheer, expressing relief that she'd managed to commit so many screw ups in *one* test instead of mangling a whole string of them, and is looking forward to her next show.

11

Tens
(With Apologies to Bo)

The scale that judges use deserves a little explanation. As you know, each number has a descriptive equivalent. Four is "Insufficient." Five, which used to translate as "Sufficient," is now going to be called "Marginal" to make you feel a little worse about getting them. Six is "Satisfactory." Seven is "Fairly Good," and so on.

It seems to me that each of the middle numbers cover a fairly wide range. There's a breadth of images and behaviors in a judge's head that register as 5s. There are Big 5s and there are Little 5s and lots of ways to get them or any of the other 5s in between. The same thing is approximately true with 6s.

But as you approach the more rarified ends of the spectrum, the bandwidth that represents a 1 or a 9 or a 10 gets much more narrow. Nobody ever talks about a Big 9, for instance. A 9 is a 9. A 10 is a 10.

As a judge, you can intellectualize and dissect a 6 or even an 8 as you give it. For me, though, a 9 or a 10 is given viscerally. The quality of the movement performed jumps out at you so obviously that it simply proclaims its excellence and the score is self-evident.

In a little less than 40 years of showing I've earned (or at least received) *one* 10. I remember it very well. I still have the test sheet. It was in the New England Championships in 1980 in a Second Level test, and it made enough difference in my score to push my horse over the top to win. The movement was a left turn in trot from E towards B, a halt at X, the move off to trot, and a right turn at B.

Even before we got our tests back, word circulated around the show grounds about that score, and it was noteworthy enough at the time that I subsequently got more than a handful of phone calls and cards in the mail mentioning it.

A funny thing—a few months later I saw my ride on video at NEDA's annual meeting, and while I liked that halt, it didn't make the earth move for me much more than some other nice 8s had along the way. Clearly it had struck the judge's fancy a bit more than it did mine.

When I was a younger judge, I had a philosophical reason for never giving 10s. I figured for them to be worth something, they really should be awarded by someone whose opinion "really mattered." In practical terms, a nice, fat 9 from me would be meaningful enough, and that was as high as my personal scale went.

This feeling was reinforced when I was sitting at lunch with five other judges at a show in Stillwater, Minnesota. The topic of 10s came up and about how rare they were until the small "r" at the table piped up, "Oh, I gave six of them this morning!"

And then there was the story of my student Eunice years ago. She had a gangly, razor-narrow Saddlebred/TBX in training with me and he knew the rudiments of dressage. He was an adequate mover at best, but he could put his nose in and more or less go forward. Eunice, who had never shown at all before, decided to take him to a very backyardy schooling Two Phase Event. It was so low-key that the organizer had hired her next door neighbor to judge the dressage, the neighbor's principal qualification being that she had ridden a test or two sometime in her life and at least knew where the letters were.

Eunice came back from her show with her test sheet in hand and asked me to look at it and tell her how she could improve. But the "judge" had given her a 95 percent! And all her scores were either 9 or 10. The best I could manage was, "Gee, Eunice, I think I'd just hang onto this one and maybe frame it 'cause you aren't likely to see another like this in the rest of your life!"

That kind of thing can happen, although usually not to this degree, when a novice "judge" in order to be kind boosts pretty bad rides into OK scores. Then when a halfway decent one comes along, they have nowhere to go with their scores but off the chart.

[By the way, now that I'm *old,* I DO give 10s or at least I've given one and I'm eagerly waiting for the next one to come along.]

12

Dismounting Without Permission
(Or Saving the Volunteers the Trouble of Taking Down the Ring)

Presumably if you realize that you aren't the only victim of an embarrassing moment, you won't live in fear that one might befall you. I can think of a few I've witnessed or been party to over the years….

Many years ago I was judging in a grass arena in Vermont. It was very early and the arena was wet with the dew. My rider was a chunky teenaged novice doing Training Test 3. The arena was made of plastic chain on stakes. Unfortunately, at the beginning of the canter her horse kicked out, got himself tangled in the chain, and bounced his rider off onto the ground. Then since he still had the chain around his leg he backed most of the way across the arena bringing it with him. The rider was flat on her stomach, tenaciously hanging onto the reins, and being dragged along as part of the package. Eventually he ran out of enthusiasm for his escapade, and the girl jumped up and started pulling the chain back across the grass towards its original location. By and by the arena got reassembled, we got her remounted, and she proceeded gamely to finish her test.

It did take a quick reading of the rulebook and a bit of interpretation to be sure that was legal. Falling off isn't cause for elimination but leaving the arena is. The question became: Is the arena defined by the chains themselves (which her horse was outside by the time he'd rearranged them) or is the arena defined by where she wished it had remained before all this happened?

In our judgment she was going to be penalized enough when her mother saw the grass stains on her white breeches so it only seemed fair to rule on the other matter in her favor.

In another arena-deconstructing episode back up north, Susan was riding a fairly obnoxious training horse—a young Morgan stallion—in his first schooling show. She was the first ride of the day and it was raining quite steadily. Consequently the judge had been placed under a large beach umbrella at a table at C. While going around the outside of the ring before his test, the Morgan took serious exception to the umbrella and shied INTO the arena. It, unfortunately, wasn't made of breakable chains but was composed of yellow nylon rope threaded through stakes that had been painstakingly pounded into the ground. Not an especially adept jumper, the horse didn't quite clear the rope and managed to remove more than half the entire arena, stakes and all, depositing them somewhere down past A. He was a less than popular competitor at that point and it took a long time in the rain for the show crew to put everything back together again.

Edgar Hotz used to tell a leaving-the-arena story. He was judging once when an inexperienced amateur rider came down the centerline, tracked to the right but only negotiated half the turn and let her horse jump out of the arena between the corner and M. To rectify the problem as best she could, Edgar said she turned her horse around pointed him at the spot where she'd left, jumped back in, but proceeded directly past his booth, and jumped right out the other side next to H!. "If at first you don't succeed…," one supposes.

While we're in the Unsolicited Exiting Department, I had a new student once upon a time, a 12-year-old Pony Clubber on a leased medium pony named Lightning. The first time I taught her was on a Thursday, two days before she was headed off to the PC dressage rally. As you can imagine, when someone is about to go competing, you don't try to change everything in one lesson. So I made some suggestions about the tempo she wanted and how to ride the figures a little better. My parting words were "Have some nice rides, bring me your test sheets, and we'll talk about things next week."

So the following Thursday it's time for her next lesson.

"Lindsay," I say, "How was the rally?"

"Not so good," she answers.

"Why?"

"My pony ran away with me."

"Oh, how far?" I ask jokingly.

"All the way home!" she moans.

Lightning had not only left the arena during his test but had left the show grounds, and cantered three miles down the road to his own barn.

The happy ending to this sad tale is that Lindsay's parents wisely bought her a different horse and she went on to be quite a successful eventor at the Prelim level, never again to pass through town in uncontrolled haste.

And finally an affair with a somewhat less sanguine outcome….

I was judging at a recognized show at the horse park in Conyers, Georgia— an old Training Level test where you took the canter on the 20-meter circle

36

between B and E. A middle-aged novice woman was in the arena on a gruesomely unpleasant Thoroughbred. As she asked for the canter, the horse got strong and started pitching. He came down the long side towards my booth getting faster and faster and spending more and more time leaping through the air. The rider did what she could but shortly was deposited heavily in the corner between H and C.

The horse left the ring and was last seen disappearing up the hill still bucking at a good clip. The rider lay there immobile. Fortunately, the EMTs arrived in about 20 seconds and found her breathing but unresponsive. In the next minutes we were joined by two police cars, a fire truck (in case she might spontaneously combust like the drummer in *Spinal Tap*, I guess), and the ambulance. Everything but a helicopter.

This involved a long delay because although she had regained consciousness, as a precaution, the techs wanted to strap her to a backboard before they transported her. The TD, meanwhile, resisted my suggestion that if we could just roll her to the inside off the track, we could go on with the class.

The woman spent the night in the local hospital for observation but was generally not much the worse for wear. I spoke to her on the phone to offer my commiserations and volunteered to send her the uncompleted test sheet (which she appreciated) that read:

6	Straight entry, haunches left in halt
6	Incomplete acceptance
7	Accurate figure, work to improve connection
5	Internalized tension
4	Explosive depart
___	Whoa, whoa! Oh, (expletive deleted)!

And a squiggly line that trailed off down the page.

13
Gone but Not Forgotten
(Little Run Run Run Runaway)

I can think of three relatively local cases where horses not only left the showgrounds but disappeared altogether. None of them was doing dressage at the time; each was on cross country where it is easier and a bit more common for the rider to part company with the saddle.

One was at a horse trials in Immokalee, Florida. A second at a schooling event in Tallahassee where a pony disappeared into a 1000-acre wood and didn't present himself again for 24 hours.

And then there was a horse that dumped its rider at the Basingstoke HT (also in rural north central Florida) and was not seen for a week till he was finally spotted and collared 15 miles from the grounds, swimming across a lake with his saddle still on.

Perhaps more amazing was a tale related by a race track friend from up in Massachusetts. When we lived up North, in the wintertime we would occasionally take our horses to Crane's Beach for a romp and a gallop in the surf.

The beach was a several mile long sandspit with no structures or marks of civilization. It was backed by dunes and a wide tidal estuary. On the ocean side the slope was very gradual and at low tide it was pockmarked by sandbars and pools, and you could stroll out a quarter of a mile from shore without the water coming up to the horses' bellies. Blue sky, sand, sunshine, and sparkling ocean. Other than the winter chill, you could hardly ask for more.

You would meet another horse person now and then or someone walking the beach on foot, but for the most part it was usually nearly deserted—producing a feeling of great solitude.

When the regular ground was frozen hard, racetrack people would sometimes take their horses to Crane's for exercise too. And it was there that one young woman out exercising a very expensive TB got herself dumped off and, much to her horror, watched him dive into the water and swim out to sea! Totally out of sight. Thoughts of how in the world she could ever explain to the horse's owner and trainer that she'd lost their horse to the fishes played through her mind when, luckily, the horse swam back into view and she was able to grab him as he waded ashore.

14
Write What I Say; Don't Write Anything Else
(Scribing Stories)

Judges really respect the volunteers who make shows possible. We know that it's the exception, not the rule, where show management can afford to pay real money for "professional" scribes. And honestly, scribing isn't that hard to do. Over all the years and dozens of scribes whom I've worked with, I think I can say that all but a few had a good time and most maybe even learned something.

First-timers usually catch on fast, and there's hardly ever a problem, but judges being human, when we get together it's easy to start telling war stories. The most famous giggle-y scribing misunderstanding (perhaps apocryphal) that judges always tell is the centerline comment "wiggles from X to C" that came out on the test sheet as "wiggles from ecstasy."

I'm not sure if that ever really happened but I know all of these did because they happened to me:

- Back in the '80s, one of my students came back from the show office with her test (Third Level), her ribbon, and a very confused look on her face. "I don't understand what this judge means," she said. The score in the block was an 8. The comment was "Good Round Bears." That one took a while to decipher, but closer examination revealed it applied to a haunches-out, a "good renvers."

- Scribes occasionally confound us. Once I invited a student of mine to come along and scribe for the day, a woman who herself had a fair amount of experience showing and presumably understood the routine. Before we began, I briefed her just to be sure, and when the first horse came down the centerline, I began my usual patter of verbiage: "Drifts slightly left into square halt, 7. Nice topline, add more thrust, 6," and so on. About half way through the test, I glanced over to ensure that she was still with me, only to discover that thus far, the paper was blank. She hadn't written a word! "Hey!" I exclaimed. "What's the matter?" "Oh," she replied rather casually, "I was just watching."

- My wife, also a judge, reported encountering just the opposite once. Her instructions to her scribe, the father of a rider and an engineer by trade who'd been recruited to help out, included showing him where the comments went and the admonition, "Be sure to write small."

  She was quite amazed as he handed her the first completed test sheet to see that he had painstakingly and neatly written every score and comment she'd given in infinitesimally small letters all in the first block!

- I hardly ever remember not being able to cope with whichever scribe was assigned to me. At one horse trial, however, I met my match. No matter how I tried to convince her, my scribe—otherwise quite a lovely lady—would not write down what I dictated to her.

  If I said "7, slightly stiff last part," she would write "7, stiff." Not exactly the same meaning as you can see. I tried shortening my comments. I tried post editing when she'd hand the sheet over, and in one case it was a good thing that I was checking.

  In a Prelim level event test, the horse was supposed to make a rising lengthening on the diagonal. My words were "6, Big, but too much on forehand." Her version was "6, Big Butt on forehand"!

- Then there's the scribe who couldn't spell. I've been known to use some obscure words—largely for my own amusement—when I judge; so it never troubles me to whisper their spelling to my scribe. One particular young lady, however, was a little more challenged in this department than normal. Like spelling that thing you do at X "hault" for instance.

  In a First Level test, one comment for a canter lengthening was "6, needs to loosen the loins."

  "How do you spell "loins?" she whispered.

  "L - O – I – N – S," I answered.

"Isn't that 'Lion'?" she asked.

"No," I said, "You spell that 'L – Y – I – N'. Don't you ever listen to country music?

OK, one last story: this one involving the late Edgar Hotz. Edgar was a highly respected Senior judge with a bit of a German accent and a rather austere demeanor. He was judging a dressage show down in the bayou country of Louisiana and had been promised a Saturday evening mudbug (crawfish) boil when the day's classes were finished.

His scribe was a sweet young ingénue who was stopped dead in her tracks when at the conclusion of the last ride, he turned to her and with no double meaning intended said, "Und ven do ve get to the pinching and sucking?"

15
Origins of the Boneless Bulldog Ranch
(Apropos of Nothing)

I can't logically rationalize including this story here, but I can't help myself. For the past 35 years—most of my adult life—I've been "doing horses": teaching riding for a living, for the past 25 or so specializing in dressage. Back in the late '80's, French Bulldogs first came into my life, Senior Bulldog Number One being a hand-me-down brindle that my wife, Susan, brought home from a meeting one blustery March night, complete with leash, blanket, and bowl. My initial uninitiated reaction was "What in the world is THAT?" and then "Who does it belong to?"

Shortly I came to understand that our gnome-faced accidental tourist was Max, and before long it became clear that we now belonged to him. That began a so-far nearly 20 year relationship with the snufflers, including three litters who have made up our extended family.

My current owner is Jake, another brindle who constantly accompanies me as I make my teaching rounds. Among dogs he's Robert Redford playing both Bob Woodard and the Sundance Kid. Athletic and debonair, he's a great listener and receives my compliments graciously. His grin puts one on my face. To me he's as charming as a little kid's stuffed toy grown up and come to life.

Recently I indulged myself in a different day-off guilty pleasure and took myself to the MacDill Airfest in Tampa. All day the air was full of the requisite skydivers, hot military jets, old biplanes, and high tech aerobatic competition craft. One brief, rather tame act that was nearly lost in the shuffle was several flybys of a lumbering old B-25, a twin engine medium bomber of a type that flew in Italy and the South Pacific during World War II.

As it made its sedate photo passes, I was reminded of a book I owned when I was a little kid, a book that I devoured over and over called **Gunner and the Dumbo**. This was a little more grown up than a "picture book," but it was extensively illustrated and clearly for pre-adolescent readers. I bet I must have read it dozens of times… enough to have practically memorized the text. This, remember, was back in the '50s when WW II was still fresh in

many minds. So it wasn't unusual that a kid's story would be written about a B-25 aircrew and their mascot, a small brown dog. In the book this little dog, Gunner, accompanies his crew everyplace… to the mess hall, to the briefings, even on the missions where he wears a custom-fitted life jacket. As I read this story as a child, I never gave much thought as to what kind of dog he was. A Boxer, I supposed, because my next door neighbor had one.

In any case, in the story the plane eventually gets shot down and the crew members find themselves floating on a raft in the Pacific. Gunner, every boy's hero, somehow knows to bark a warning when his sensitive ears pick up the sound of enemy patrol planes. And likewise he recognizes the sound of the searching American seaplane, the "Dumbo," that spots them and swoops down for the rescue.

These memories came flooding came back to me as I watched the B-25 at that air show, and I resolved to Google the book title when I got home that night. Well, in fact, the book does still exist and it was available at several

Steve Waller

used book sellers and on eBay. But most startling and electrifying were the on-line illustrations revealing Gunner as not just any little brown dog but a brindle French Bulldog—exactly like my best pals, first Max, then Augie, and now Jake who've been my shadows these last 20 years.

Just now, at age 60, I've discovered that as a 10-year-old, I had "met" and become entranced by my best friends 30 years before I ever found them in person!

16
If a Tree Falls in the Forest…
(Thoughts on "Attention")

I always tell riders that dressage training is full of dichotomies, of paradoxes. In the Collective Marks under Submission, for example, we read that the horses are supposed to be "attentive." That's not so hard to accomplish by itself. You can usually intimidate your horse into listening to you. It might be crude. It might take the sword dangling over his head, but you can get him to take notice! But that same paragraph on the tests demands that the horse be "confident." This might be a little more difficult to achieve, but with some work, you can usually get him to be confident. Face it, a horse dragging you around on his forehand may be perfectly confident. The complication is in combining these two seemingly contrary qualities. "Attentive" and "Confident" together is a higher hurdle to surmount.

So what does it mean for your horse to be attentive? If he's massively late and sluggish to the leg (dialup instead of broadband) or if he keeps cruising on inertia and momentum when you try to make a downward transition, the diagnosis is obvious. But if you've never ridden a really well-trained dressage horse who is tuned and on the aids, it can be a bit harder to know if your horse is fulfilling all his responsibilities to you.

It isn't unusual for a rider with a Training Level perspective to assume that if his horse is trotting around with his nose in, he's paying attention. However, I try to make a distinction between "Passive Acceptance" and "Active Acceptance." The former can include all varieties of coasting, drifting, cruising, and posing. And if the horse is a nice enough mover, the judges will sometimes tolerate this or, at least at the lower levels, not punish it too severely.

Active Acceptance includes more than attentiveness—topics for later times—but it MUST include realtime responsiveness. Imagine sitting at your computer and moving the mouse on its pad. If everything's working correctly, the cursor on the screen will move instantaneously and in complete concert with the mouse. Consider that your horse's center of gravity should be as maneuverable in as timely a manner.

If you're accustomed to less than total responsiveness, you might be surprised how much a really trusting and trained horse can "take" without it scaring him. Good upper level horses aren't supposed to be flighty, but they are supposed to be "hot/quick" to the aids. Think of a tonic bottle that's been sitting in the fridge that still makes a pffizzzz when you unscrew it.

It should do this every time. If not, you pitch it out and get a new bottle. With your horse, you don't toss him. You fix him. It's more like putting a new CO_2 cartridge into the seltzer bottle. Recharge him! Keep the pffizzzz there.

Dressage training is soooo much about communication, about discerning whether you're conducting a truly interactive, footfall-by-footfall dialogue with your horse. By asking him the right questions you can detect if he's really making himself available to you. When I coach and teach, I ask my students to guard against perfunctory, rote responses from their horses—not to let their horses "mail it in." I keep emphasizing phrases to them like "Keep him *honest*," "Make his response *sincere*," "Make each step *valid*," and that great caution from the paranoid Reagan administration *"Trust but Verify."*

The timing and coordination of the aids is central to them working correctly. A late or non-answer to any one aid messes up that timed coordination completely. Only by constantly checking that the relationship is "real," deep enough, and confidently reactive can you be sure that the aids will produce the result they're meant to.

17

It Figures
(What Goes Around Is Supposed to Come Around)

As you no doubt have read, when the National Foundation for Obsessive Compulsive Disorder was looking for a poster child, the first thing they did was contact the USDF to obtain a roster of our members.

Because dressage seems to attract so many of that ilk, it is sometimes hard to tell whether your instructor is "just having another episode" or if what he's so overwrought about *really* does matter as much as he insists it does.

Case in point: arena figures. At least as much as anyone, I constantly remind my students not to make corners on their circles, not to ride circles with flat sides, not to let their horses fall through the corners, and so on, figure by figure and day after day.

As a faithful Lindgren disciple, when worst comes to worst, I haul out my cones and make students think of the four points of the circle (north, east, south, and west) and if that still doesn't do it, the northeast, southeast, etc. ones in between. This is for a couple of reasons. The first is simply behavioral. If you don't tell your horse what to do, he'll just make up something on his own, and most likely his idea will involve less useful work than your idea would. Second, keeping your horse in balance is all about keeping his attention. Another way to say that is keeping your horse attentive is step by step maintaining and adjusting his balance. It works both ways.

Longitudinal balance will change gradually as your horse develops, but for the most part, lateral balance is something you should be seeking right from the start. If you make goal-less amorphous figures, you aren't apt to notice the loss of lateral balance when it occurs. It's just so easy for a circle to turn into an agreeable egg without you even being aware unless you proactively arrange rigorous and correct figures—first in your mind and later over the ground— for your horse to follow. If you want your horse to drift over his shoulder and coast around like his brain is flat-lining, ride bad figures.

Like shooting a space probe to a distant planet, a very small course correction early avoids the need for a much larger correction later on. Only by planning and visualizing the line you mean to follow (as much as 90 degrees of arc before the fact) and making small, timely adjustments can you keep your horse in balance without having to make an ungainly, rhythm-disrupting intervention that could have been avoided.

18
0.5 Halts
(Don't Rein On My Parade)

Major Lindgren used to complain about instructors who use the expression "half halt with the outside rein" or "half halt with the inside hand." He often refused to use the term "half halt" at all, preferring the advice "rebalance him" or "rock him back", because he said the term "half halt" just focused most amateur riders on their hands to solve all their problems rather than the hands being just one lesser component of the true seat/leg-originated half halt.

If pressed, he might say to "half halt *into* the rein," but the emphasis was always on the pushing aids to institute the exercise and then a nearly-but-not-quite simultaneous application of a momentarily non-allowing hand to modify or explain the push.

When he wanted to speak of rein actions, he used the more European term "parade," which he pronounced the way a Kennedy would: "pa RAHd." He explained that it came from the same root as the fencing term "to parry," and in his version of English, his command sometimes came out "Parry your horse!" If you're at all familiar with fencing, parrying is a lateral or twisting wrist motion that doesn't involve thrusting your epee forward or pulling it back. So it is with the action of the hand when you make the parade.

It must be embedded in human nature to solve things with the hands (apologies to David Beckham, et al). The horse is strong or out of balance. The student tries to make a half halt; he pulls. It doesn't work, he pulls harder.

Then I ask him to imagine a tennis date in which he gets to the court early but his partner hasn't arrived yet. So to warm up, he bounces the ball at his waist and bangs it against the green backboard at the rear of the court, the one with the white, net-high stripe painted on it. The ball caroms back to him and he smacks it at the wall again.

Now, here comes the dressage analogy: If you want the ball to bounce back farther, you don't change the backboard. A wall is a wall. Instead, you whack the ball with that much more authority at it. And that is the way of half halts. The wall is your hand—momentarily non-allowing when you make a parade with it. The energy-infusing racquet is like your driving aids. Add to them *and it makes the half halt larger.*

To make effective parades, you have to do them without pulling back with your hands. That's what Major Lindgren was trying to get across. To help explain, I remind my students about the particulars of the Salem Witch Trials. I ask them to picture the stocks that errant women were placed in on the town green in those colonial times. I propose to create for them a stock-like device that would sit on their horse's withers in front of the saddle. Once the upper branch of the stock is hinged down into place, the wrist holes would be just large enough for the rider to take up whatever slack might be in the reins through his elbows. But when the time comes to make a parade, the arm could move back no further, and the take-give/resist-soften motion would have to be made entirely within the wrist and fingers.

It's worth noting that aside from their function within the coordinated execution of a half halt, the rider's hands are permitted to do a variety of other (hopefully) subtle things. The gentle, intermittent massage of the horse's mouth, the maintenance of a pliable, lubricated poll and jaw, the occasional positioning or counter-positioning of his head are all things that your hands do in vibrations (the "palsy rein"), in squeezes (the lime in the Corona or, when mandated, the crushing of the aluminum beer can), or in rotations ("turning the key in the lock").

As Frau Rosemary Springer, a German dressage star from the 1960s, once said to me, "Quiet hands are good but don't think "quiet" means DEAD!"

19
Limits
(Thinking Inside the Box)

"Running through the hand," "Against the bit," "Using the Fifth Leg." We've all heard those phrases and most of us at one time or another have had them directed AT us.

Having your horse moving nicely on contact should be reminiscent of your small dog obediently at heel on his leash. It shouldn't feel like being dragged down the sidewalk on your stomach by two Great Danes who just spied the neighbor's cat. The leash is supposed to establish a limit that the dog respects; it's not supposed to be like a heavy cable that ties down a ship in a gale.

Using a choke collar on a big dog is supposed to work the same way. If it's actually choking him—if he's turning some various shades of purple and gasping for breath—forget it. It's not sending the message it's designed to. I'm reminded of a flamboyant baseball umpire who was very prominent back when I was growing up, a guy named Jocko Conlan. Conlan was small of stature but quite a commanding presence. His nemesis was Leo Durocher, a hotheaded redneck manager who was quick to start a rhubarb if things weren't going his team's way. Leo would inevitably storm out of the dugout and go toe to toe with the ump, his hat turned backwards on his head, spittle flying from his jaw as he screamed invectives. Conlan would give Durocher a chance to vent, but if he got too carried away or didn't wind himself down in due course, Conlan would step back a pace and draw a line in the infield dirt with his spiked toe. Then he'd walk away and call over his shoulder, "Leo, cross that line and you're out of this game!"

That's the principle of setting limits to behaviors. Whether we're speaking of gross, large scale behaviors or miniscule deviations from balance and attention, impressing on students the idea of setting limits for their horses is monumentally important.

Here's one more example. The picture says it all. This is a "bottomless cart" being used to shift these German cows from a pasture on one side of town to a place within walking distance but somewhat removed from their point of origin. As the sides of the pen move along over the road, the cows respect the boundaries they define and walk along within the space without the sides ever touching them.

This is how your horse ought to relate to your aids—surrounded but not physically held, respecting the limits enough that they choose not to challenge them, staying *agreeably inside the box*.

20
Centers of Gravity:
Moving the Mass

When I lived in Boston, it was hard not to be a Celtics fan. Those were the days of the Big Three—Larry Byrd, Kevin McHale, and Robert Parrish—and even if the team didn't always win a championship, they were always very, very good. One year the Celts were due to play Michael Jordan and the Chicago Bulls in the playoffs, and one of the sportscasters was interviewing Dennis Johnson, the Celtics top defender, when DJ said a very dressage-like thing.

DJ was going to have to guard Michael, and the question was "How do you stop him?"

DJ's answer, "Well, I can't look at Michael Jordan's eyes, 'cause he can throw a headfake on me, go backdoor, and I'm standing there flatfooted.

"And I can't look at his shoulders, 'cause if I try to follow them, he'll drop one, spin, and drive right by me.

"But," smiled DJ, "What I have to do is guard his belt buckle. 'Cause wherever that goes, the rest of Michael has to go there too."

In that little soliloquy Dennis Johnson was speaking directly to people who hang on the inside rein overbending the neck to the inside and then wonder why the horse bulges out of the circle.

Horses won't necessarily go where their nose points, but if you always focus on getting their center of gravity (approximately the area above the girth and between your thighs) tracking where you want—just like Michael Jordan's belt buckle—the rest of your horse simply has to go along. Then you can think of his alignment or bending to suit whatever movement or figure you're trying to perform.

Along similar lines, I recall teaching a surgeon in some clinics back in the day. He owned an upper level schoolmaster and often fell into the same override- with-the-inside-rein trap, letting his horse escape through the outside shoulder with great frequency.

He was a nice guy but a little full of himself. Drove a Porsche. Trophy wife. Serious white-columned mansion replete with restaurant-style kitchen, wine cellar, media center with theater seats and a viewing screen that covered the wall. Even a workout room on the third floor and an elevator to get to it.

Marnie Hutcheson

After one trying lesson, I said to him, "Doc, you know what you need for your place to improve your riding?"

A pause. Then, "Chickens!"

"Why in the world do I need chickens?" he asked me.

"Because," I explained, "when you try to turn your horse, it's like running through the flock and scattering the hens. You need to get a half-dozen chickens for the driveway, and every night when you get home from the hospital, practice herding them around like you're using your outside aids. That's how you need to turn your horse."

I didn't understand this as a priority when I first started my (primitive) teaching career some 38 years ago. As a typical beginner instructor of that era, I knew slightly more than the people I was teaching, and I only knew rather superficial, obvious things. One obvious, visible concept is to keep the horses bent to the inside, and that was something that I really harped on back then. Of course, I am still very interested in bending, but with green or evasive problem-practiced horses, it just isn't the most important thing until other problems have been addressed. That's when it's time to remember DJ's formula or to get out there and herd those chickens!

Let Only the Truth Be Spoken ....
"Son, you can't handle the truth."

It's easy to tire of those self-important bios that clinicians supply to clinic organizers. Here is a bio I provided to the Dallas Dressage Club to publicize a clinic I was doing for them.

Bill Woods Biographical Information
compiled by Sidd Finch

Bill Woods (not his real name) comes to the Dallas area several times a year. He and his wife, Onyx, are members of the Federal Dressage Witness Protection Program; thus, their true place of residence is unknown. Both train and compete most of the year in central Florida, often in disguise.

Bill has been teaching in Texas since the mid '80s, having been brought here by Lisa Brown. They had met in New Hampshire some years before, drawn together by a mutual love of hybrid roses that they tended on summer afternoons at the institution. Lisa, whom DDC veterans may remember, reminded many of us of current club member Lisa Avila, only on 78 rpm.

Orphaned at an early age and left to roam the gutters of Darien, CT— forced to collect aluminum cans and discarded cigar butts to pay for his classical dressage education—Bill nonetheless rose rapidly in his chosen discipline. He went to his first Olympic Games in 1976, sitting near the top of the bleachers right behind letter S.

Bill attended many National Instructors' Seminars through the 1980s, and when it became apparent he would never get it right, was made a member of its staff. Recruited by Lowell Boomer to head the born-again (it had croaked in 1978 after a brief and bloody false start) Instructor/Trainer Council, he spent seven years dutifully passing the ammunition as the USDF shot itself in the foot.

Now devoting much of his time to monk-like contemplation, judging, and other scholarly endeavors, he emerges from seclusion periodically to monitor the progress of his Texas students. Usually he sits quietly in a helium-filled glass booth, gazing serenely through his spectacles, occasionally summoning a rider to offer cryptic advice, sometimes in English, but more often in unintelligible grunts or in a high-pitched whistle audible only to dogs. His students report that their horses go lighter, with more engagement and self-carriage. One woman swears that the lumps on her head have gone away.

Bill welcomes auditors at his clinics but requests that you turn off all portable electronic devices and leave any large magnets at home.

22

Siddhartha, Won't You Please Come Home?
(Department of Further Explanations)

You might have noticed that the previous bio was attributed to Sidd Finch. Those of you who were *au courant* 25 years ago and for whom the clock stopped immediately thereafter, recognize him as the character George Plimpton invented for a famous *Sports Illustrated* April Fool's Day spoof.

In Plimpton's totally straight-faced, deadpan article, Sidd Finch was a New York Mets minor league phenom who, with a pitching-machine-like, stiff armed delivery, could throw a baseball 168 mph. In the story, the Mets were keeping Sidd's skills under wraps, but he was known to wear only one shoe while on the mound, to have attended Harvard where his only possessions were a rice bowl and a prayer rug, and to have "perfect pitch."

At the time, Susan and I were editing the New England Dressage Association's newsletter, which we did with tongue planted firmly in cheek. Sidd never did pitch in the Majors, but when he disappeared from the pages of *SI,* we invited him to join our staff as guest editor. Whenever we wanted to express an outlandish or potentially controversial opinion, we'd let Sidd write the story. New Englanders, to say nothing of New England dressage people, being what they are, many readers just assumed that Sidd Finch really existed and even wrote "Dear Mr. Finch" letters to him care of us.

Sidd not only contributed the bio above, but nearly made it into print much more recently. Susan, who has been known to don her Strident Environmentalist hat and devolve into letter writing frenzies, penned a submission off to the

Ocala Star Banner, and because letter writers may only be published once a month, signed Sidd's name to it. The editor, however, was an *SI* reader with a good memory, and although he admired Sidd greatly, suggested Susan had better wait till the end of the month and use her own name to get her letter in the paper.

23
Workshop Encounters

Back in the mid 1980s I was tapped by Lowell Boomer and the staff of the National Instructors Seminar to conduct weekend Instructor Workshops around the country—to bring Hopkins Seminar philosophy and methodology to the so-called "grassroots." A few years later my wife, who had attended the weeklong seminar several times, was also invited to conduct workshops and occasionally we did team teaching together.

I would hope that we did some good in the 50 or so workshops we conducted. They spanned the country from Alaska, California, and Arizona to Texas, Kansas, and Illinois to New York, North Carolina, and Florida. But along the way we certainly encountered some interesting people and events. A few qualified as real doozies.*

In general, the format was built around some lecture theory and some teaching that we did of the Participating Instructors on their own horses, but the centerpiece was the "PI's" practice teaching of assigned topics that they performed with demonstration riders and then were critiqued as the entire group discussed their lessons.

It was here that we ran into some unusual situations.

---

* If you ever encountered an aged grandparent or similarly ancient individual using that term "doozie" and wondered where it came from, I can tell you on best authority that it originated with the Duesenberg, which back in the 1930s was the equivalent standardbearer of automotive excellence to today's Mercedes/BMW/Cadillac/Lexus. A "doozie" was something very cool.

Out in California we were conducting one workshop before a fairly large audience—maybe 75 watchers—and one of our demo riders was a rather staid—dare I say "stuffy"—middle-aged DQ who was fairly notorious in that area for all the reasons that her station in life might suggest. She was trying to make a leg yield with only marginal success when she blurted out to the group, "I feel like I'm on a drunken sailor!"

There was a brief silence that shortly degenerated into our inviting her to fill in the details of when she had last done that and just exactly what it had felt like to be aboard one.

The demo horses and riders were always provided by the organizers, and while they were representative of what the local instructors had to deal with, they didn't always make dressage lessons easy. On the first afternoon of a three-day workshop, we and the PIs would meet all the demo riders and find out just what they could and couldn't do.

Down in the Paul Prudhomme bayou country of Louisiana I was doing a workshop, and one demo pair particularly caught my attention. The horse was a weedy, extremely wild-eyed chestnut Thoroughbred, his rider a chunky middle-aged guy with a long, bushy beard.

"So, John," I began. "Tell us what you've been working on with your horse."

"Wahl," he replied, "Ah mostly do Civil War re-enactments and Ah bin trying to git him more used to the cannons."

Practice Teaching sessions had a way of leaving me nearly speechless, but in one instance I found my voice in the nick of time. At another Down South and out in the countryside venue, I had assigned a PI to do a basic warm-up and suppling session with two novice riders in a semi-private lesson. The PI was a nice guy who had recently arrived from Europe with the very best of classical intentions. His guinea pigs were two very nervous and nearly helpless ladies. One was mounted on a prancing, extremely inside out Thoroughbred just off the track; the other was riding a highly defensive and suspicious former hazing horse. (That's what they call a rodeo horse whose rider's job is to gallop beside a steer to keep him running straight so the bulldogger can leap onto the steer's neck and wrestle him to the ground.)

The instructor had just finished making a polite and formal introduction to them when he said, "Now cross your stirrups over the withers and take the track in sitting trot one behind the other."

"Omigosh," thought I. This was clearly an appropriate time to find my voice and an intervention ensued before any carnage took place.

Then there was Dick. He was a cowboyish older gentleman who had some ideas about horse training and was a PI at a workshop being held in the northwoods. Anything that he lacked in technical acumen, he tried to more than make up for with a somewhat larger than life self-generated persona.

This particular workshop was located near a "little town that time forgot" that could have emerged straight from a Garrison Keillor story, and the local high school cheerleaders were catering all the lunches to pay for their trip to cheerleading camp later in the summer.

The irrepressible Dick was slated to do the first practice teaching session after the noon meal, and as I waited for the girls to fry my burger at the lunch stand, I said to them, "So do you guys know any dressage cheers?"

They had been hanging out and watching most of the morning so they said, "Sure. What would you like?"

I explained that Dick would be next and that it might be nice to start his lesson with a cheer to get everyone in the right mood. So about a half hour later with the audience arrayed down the long side of the arena and Dick ready to start, the nine cheerleaders jogged into the ring hands on hips, lined themselves up on the quarterline, divided the watchers into two groups, and displaying fancy footwork and pom pom-wielding moves, led everyone in a rousing

"Get Your Horse!"............ "In Front of the Leg!"

Back in California at the same "drunken sailor workshop" described earlier, we had another strange moment. A woman named Tina was being an especially passive, wisp of a demo rider and her PI was trying with limited success to get Tina to keep her horse on an accurate circle. The instructor had a similarly soft and passive sort of approach, and the horse kept bulging off across the ring with his rider doing very little to prevent him.

Susan and I were co-conducting the session and sitting with the rest of the spectators but fairly far apart. With no rehearsal or pre-arrangement, we stood up in unison and shouted stridently, "TINA!!! TURNER!!!"

At that, Tina shook off her cobwebs and made her horse turn.

24

Is *Any*body Listening?
More on "Attention"

I keep coming back to this theme over and over because so many riders just don't seem to know how much their horse is supposed to be listening to them and what they should expect to do to create and maintain that relationship.

Cut-throaty eventing kids basically "get" it, but not former equitation riders and not a lot of late-to-dressage amateur adults.

Back in the mid-'70s, a colleague and I were conducting an afternoon dressage program for the riding club at the University of Rhode Island. She had brought her horse and was going to do a demo that I would narrate. Then I would teach a sample dressage lesson to six chosen riders from the club mounted on university school horses while the rest of the members watched. When it came time for the lesson, I was presented with a motley gang of relatively clueless horses and riders. Most could at least navigate, but one in particular kept ending up beside me in the center of the arena whenever I turned my back. So I got on this horse in the lesson and yielded him around a bit, got him moving off my leg (despite a few objections), and handed him back to his rider. I was so pleased when she was then able to keep him on the rail and going at the speed she chose. "What a good example of the benefits of putting a horse on the aids," I was thinking when a member of the audience raised her hand.

"Excuse me, Mr. Woods?"

"Yes?"

"Um, are you really a dressage rider?"

"Well, yes," I replied. "I'd like to think so. Why?"

"I've *seen* dressage," she said. "I've seen it at Madison Square Garden, and it didn't look like *that!*"

Of course Grand Prix ought to look elegant, but when people want the veneer of Grand Prix when the horses aren't remotely on any aids, that's an Emperor's New Clothes moment. The message is: establish the basic relationships and use them to progressively develop the horse, both mentally and physically, to fulfill the heightened requirements level by level.

As I used to point out at Instructor Workshops, we have one set of overriding goals but "There Are Many Roads to Rome" because if you're coming from England, you take a different path than if you're coming from Greece. Or Carthage. Or Wherever.

Another attention-related image for you: Picture a glass of freshly brewed homemade iced tea. Not the Southern kind with a ton of boiled up sugar water mixed in from the get-go, but the unsweetened kind that you squeeze your own lemon slice into and into which you dump a couple of sugar packets and with a long-handled spoon stir like crazy. If you set the glass

on the counter and go off for a while, when you come back the tea will still be a little sweet, but a lot of the sugar will have settled into the bottom of the glass like an undersea sand dune.

If you're going to drink the tea intermittently and not gulp it down all at once, you have to keep that spoon handy and every so often re-stir the tea to keep all that sugar in suspension.

And that's what you have to remember to do with your horse. Remember to keep stirring. Don't let his consciousness settle to the bottom of the glass where you can't taste it.

Less charitably, I've heard the horse be compared to an aerosol paint can. That little marble in the bottom of the can is his brain. Your job is to be sure that marble will rattle around and not get mired in the sludge. If you can't "hear the rattle," your horse has zoned out under you.

One more thought on attention: The way you access "attention" varies with a horse's temperament that, in turn, is somewhat related to his breed type. A hot horse (which we think of stereotypically as a Thoroughbred or Arab type) needs to slow his mental pinwheels down enough to be able to concentrate on the messages you're trying to send.

The way you arrive at attention with a warmblood is sometimes the same but often it's like coming from the opposite end of the spectrum. Some warmbloods veg out way past cold-blooded horses. They act like real *cold-blooded animals*. You know how in the wintertime a snake's or a lizard's body temp goes down? Its metabolism slows, and it semi-hibernates.

If, heaven forbid, your warmblood acts this way, then you need to get him much quicker to the aids—alert, alive, and reactive. You certainly don't want your un-warm warmblood to be accused of having a dreaded case of REPTILE DYSFUNCTION, do you?

25
A Cabaret, a Box of Chocolates, or What?
Life on the Dressage Road

There's lots of weird stuff waiting to be discovered out there on the road. I'm certainly not the only person ever to have noticed that!

When you teach, you get to do a bunch of other stuff, too. Some clinicians may be able to fold their wings over their eyes and hang upside down in the dark till the next day's lessons begin, but then you miss half the fun!

"Utah" is the punchline in this one. The story begins with a clinic's potluck supper. These aren't all that rare. You teach for the day and then Saturday night everyone gets together for a meal they all provide, you watch some videos, tell some stories, and crank up for Sunday. Usually, the dinners are fairly organized. If there isn't a formal sign up sheet, various riders are recruited to a) bring the entrée or b) bring a salad or c) bring a dessert, and so on. If the organizer is especially venturesome, they might leave things to chance. Most places the law of averages would save them, and magically a reasonable variety of dishes would arrive. Not this one time in Utah, however. At one clinic, aside from a small package of KFC, everybody managed to bring melon balls. A repast

somewhat lacking after a long day in the arena, it spurred me to post a revised Food Pyramid on the bulletin board the next time I visited.

The new pyramid showed the base of the pyramid as "Meat and Potatoes." Then came "Beer." The pyramid narrowed through other foods, and at the tiniest little tip were the melon balls. In case anyone had missed the point.

Before we leave Utah, I should mention my surprise and gratitude that Jello salads were not on the menu that night. You might already know that more Jello is consumed per capita in Utah than anywhere else in the U.S. Salt Lake City is even the site of the Jello Museum. In case you weren't aware, Mormons have a thing about Jello. Jello with marshmallows, Jello with fruit cocktail, Jello with julienne carrots, Jello with almost anything. Green Jello appears to be the hue of choice.

It was rumored that while John McCain promised to bring integrity to the Republican Party and Rudy Guliani offered to bring economic expertise, Mitt Romney said he'd bring a Jello salad.

Aside from the Jello Museum, my travels have taken me to (or near) a number of other shrines of note. The Spam Museum is in Minnesota. So is the Strip Mining Hall of Fame. As is the World's Largest Hockey Stick that I saw in person. Unfortunately, the year before it had fallen over and the little town of Eveleth had not yet raised the funds to set it back up on its blade. I had to see it side on, looking a bit like a wooden Berlin Wall, and taking up most of the downtown park it was supposed to be erected in.

Minnesotans also proudly display a colossal monument to rampant deforestation, a giant statue of Paul Bunyan and Babe the Blue Ox—a sure stop on any diligent dressage clinician's itinerary. Note that I did not see the Bemidji Paul or the Klamath, California one, but I did see the Brainerd, Minnesota Paul, which bests the others by his ability to "talk" to you.

Places I mean to go but haven't: the Museum of Bad Art in Boston, and the Mike the Headless Chicken Festival in Fruita, Colorado. I would have attended the Elvis Festival in Collingwood, Ontario (featuring 4000 paid Elvises, the famed Flying Elvises and as many as 120,000 pretenders) but it was happening the weekend after I left.

In my quasi-professional role as entertainee, I've been taken to a classical guitar recital at the Teatro Nacional de Costa Rica, to the Who at the Cotton Bowl, down the Class 5 rapids at Niagara Falls on a jetboat, disco rollerskating, bowling (where I discovered I'm no better than I was in Cub Scouts), and to a place—seriously—that you really should see, the Mustangs at Las Colinas outside Dallas. These nine far-larger-than-life bronzes cavort across a plaza fountain, splashing as though through a prairie stream. Their expressions and their muscling are exquisite. The detail is carried all the way to the soles of their feet which include sculpted frogs. The best time to view the mustangs is in the evening when they're spot lit, the plaza is uncrowded, and you can spend time absorbing their ambiance and running your hands over them.

26
"Inside, Outside, Outside"
(Not Just for Memorizing Hunter Courses)

Every cliché has a large element of truth to it. That's how they got to be clichés in the first place. Dressage clichés are no exception, and one most noteworthy example is "Ride your horse from the inside leg to the outside hand." I wouldn't begin to argue the veracity of this statement, but I have

noticed how many times it is misunderstood or misapplied. So many horses get blocked by or stuck against the outside hand. Another whole bunch get rammed through the outside rein, through the outside shoulder, and off into space.

A helpful modification to this advice I've heard attributed to Karl Mikolka. He (or someone) says to ride your horse from the inside leg *to the outside leg* to the outside hand.

If you picture your inside leg like a flashlight beaming its rays straight through the horse's barrel at the girth, then the outside leg is like a mirror placed at a 45 degree angle that redirects the beam longitudinally forward into the bit on the outside. This image keeps the horse more between your legs where he won't bulge out and reminds you to think of your *receiving* hand with the horse stretching forward into it. It makes much more sense to think of making the connection this way.

27

Say Something Once, Why Say It Again?
On Judging Attitudes

"The judge's job is not an easy one!" Well, maybe I lied. I mean all you have to do is stay alert, honest, and accurate—typical Boy Scout-ish behaviors—and deliver the news with equanimity and as helpfully as possible to the people you judge.

I like to think judges have some ancillary duties. These include trying to keep the mood light and loose and enjoyable for all concerned. This certainly doesn't preclude getting the numbers right and calling each shot as you see them. But it ought to rule out grumpy, imperious, take-this-five-as-a-gift-from-me obnoxious judging. Yes, I understand there's a lot of pressure when you're upholding the honor of your country at the Olympics, but face it, that's not the nature of most competitions. It isn't supposed to be a miserable, cut-throat kind of faceoff against hated foes. It's really you and your horse competing against an ideal, and whoever comes closest to achieving that ideal is the one that gets the blue ribbon.

A lot of riders, if we are to believe the surveys, enter tests for the feedback—to find out where they stand in their training, to find out if they're on the right track. So with all this in mind, I want riders as they pass by C awaiting the duck's call to begin to know I want them to succeed and that they should relax and enjoy what they're paying for. I can't imagine wanting to spend hundreds of dollars on entries, stabling, lodging, food, and diesel plus the built-in hassles of being away for a whole weekend just for the privilege of being abused, degraded, and made to feel stupid!

Event riders, at least the ones who are sincerely trying to get it right, seem to have a better idea of how to relate to their dressage. Olympic medalist Karen O'Conner once rode a fairly bad lower level event test in front of me. At its conclusion she stopped at G, saluted, smiled sheepishly, and said, "Do you think I could do it again with his head down?"

We understand that what judges write on the tests both block by block and in the Collectives carries a lot of weight with most riders who get their sheets back.

One thing I find to be very tedious is judges who use exactly the same limited vocabulary over and over to rider after rider and to the same rider through all that person's tests over the course of a show. I appreciate the argument that riders should know the meaning of the technical terms, and at judges' forums we all try very hard to say incredibly pithy, jargony things when we're called upon. But in real life, I think it's better to say what amounts to the same thing six different ways than to say it the same way six different times. For example, "off balance," "leaning," "hanging on inner rein," "popping the shoulder," "bulging," "overbent laterally," and "falling through the outside leg" are all ways to describe the same malady. If one phrase doesn't spark the rider's imagination to make an adjustment, hopefully another one will.

I sometimes think those little precis we write under the Collectives sound like the messages in fortune cookies.

Once at a Chinese restaurant I actually got a real dressage fortune after I finished my Kung Pao chicken. It said: "AVOID MISUNDERSTANDING WITH CALM, POISE, AND BALANCE."

Another time I got one that said: "YOU WILL HAVE RECURRING DREAMS THAT MEAN NOTHING AT ALL." I haven't yet found an occasion to put that on someone's test sheet.

A seriously-meant comment that I once wrote on somebody's sheet was: "Your horse is ruly and combobulated, but he needs to be more daisical." It seemed to "say it all" and was designed to make the rider bother to decipher it and then stop and think it over.

Another time I was judging a particularly horrible test. The horse was massively above the bit throughout and the rider, though unable to fix it at the time, certainly knew she had a problem. After her final halt she shrugged apologetically and I consoled her by saying, "Well, on the bright side, if we have a flood, he's going to be the last to drown!"

I never mind if a rider approaches me afterwards (yeah, with the TD's permission and all that) to ask about what I've written. Once after I judged at Wellington, I received a very nice e-mail from a novice Training Level competitor who wrote approximately:

Dear Mr. Woods,

I appreciated your comments and I always review my test sheets and look at them along with the videos of my rides. You judged me in Training Test 4, and there were a couple of comments you made which I didn't understand.

You said that my loop needed to be more 'zaftig' and you also said that my horse needed to learn 'to think inside the box.' Can you explain those things to me?

I was happy to write back and we exchanged several short notes. I explained that *zaftig* is a Yiddish word that could better describe Dolly Parton than Cher and it related to the shape of her ring figure and its lack of curves and bend changes. The other, of course, was a play on that "Think Outside the Box" mantra that motivational speakers and politicians always use. In this case "Inside the Box" meant keeping him more surrounded by leg and hand and in balance between them.

A few paragraphs ago I said I was always glad to talk to the riders and, presumably, their coaches. I need to relate one incident that turned out to be a notable exception. The test in question was performed by a young teenager at a schooling show. It was Training Test 1 or 2, as I recall. The girl could make some approximation of ring figures, but her horse wasn't on the aids in the conventional sense and her score, a 53 percent, reflected that.

As I broke for lunch, the show manager asked if I would be willing to talk to the girl's trainer. Naturally I agreed with the expectation of explaining to them the kind of changes in the horse's outline and balance that would let me reward the rider with higher scores.

The trainer marched up to me, held up the test, and said, "You're using all the wrong words!"

"Excuse me?"

"This doesn't make any sense. You're using all the wrong words," she said again.

I reiterated why the score was a 53 and what it meant.

The trainer in a tone of exasperation interrupted, "But you keep saying the horse should be "round."

"Yes?"

"Well, there's nothing printed on here about having to be round!"

Whereupon I launched into a brief recitation of The Object and General Principles from the Rulebook with some references to Suppleness, Submisson, and so on. It did no good.

"But it isn't required on the test," she nearly wailed.

I called all my experience into the defense of my position—all the hundreds of tests I've ridden, the thousands that I've judged, the hundreds of students that I've coached, and the standards that have been universally applied in all those cases for all these 35 years. In her mind it was an argument that I was destined to lose.

I could only hope that someday she would say to herself, "Ohhhhh......."

28

Plane Facts
A Non-Dressage Interlude

There are things in my life that are worth knowing even if they aren't directly related to dressage. As you're probably aware, I invented the Internet. I had to run from sniper fire when I visited Bosnia on a dressage fact-finding mission. And I went for one hellacious seaplane ride that I am better able to document than either of the aforementioned matters.

Her name is Cindy. Put her together with my wife and you immediately recognize trouble the same as when you see survivalists start playing with fertilizer and diesel fuel.

66

Once I had to leave town while Cindy was visiting from up North. My parting words to Susan were, "No matter what, you absolutely MAY NOT buy a pot-bellied pig or a donkey while I'm gone."

Clearly I was too specific because when I returned from my weekend clinic, her first inquiry was, "Can you hook up the trailer?" On my departure I had neglected to add, "And please don't look in the Want Advertiser and find an ancient, lame, Percheron broodmare named Babe."

On another visit of Cindy's when I had to leave town, I tried to cover all the bases and demanded, "DO NOT buy any living thing while I'm away." I came back to find they'd purchased a trampoline.

Would it be an exaggeration to call Susan's friend a bit of a free spirit?

This past winter she brought her horse to Florida and spent several months out of the New England deepfreeze training and showing with her coach from Maine. They were staying near Daytona with Race Week, Bike Week, Spring Break, and all those other Chamber of Commerce/ Chamber of Mischief happenings to tempt their not-so-Puritan souls. This afforded Cindy the opportunity to dress up and attend a Faux Biker Ball. We know it was "faux" because, one, there weren't any bikers there. And it was held at an art museum—Clue Number Two. The evening featured an auction—all for a good cause—and partly from the spirit of charitable contribution and mostly from the effect of the Chardonnay, Cindy was the final and successful bidder on a seaplane ride. Her intention was to share it with her husband who was coming to Florida to join in her 50th birthday celebration—her self-styled "Fiftieth Jubilee."

Only after she had won this "treat" did it occur to her that in partaking of this adventure she would place her queasy stomach and sensitive equilibrium in serious jeopardy. So I became her stand-in.

I was expecting something pretty tame—a fat little low-powered thing with pontoons hanging off the bottom. What I got was a very hot boat hull and an e-ticket ride. At one point we were blazing across the savannah, the airspeed indicator reading 105 knots, Neil Young blasting in the headphones. I said to our pilot, "What's our altitude right now?"

His reply confirmed my suspicions: "Six feet!"

Later we made a below-treetop-level slalom up the narrow, sinuous St. Johns River as the photo here attests, the highlight being the look on a fisherman's face as we breezed by his skiff barely above the water's surface.

It is said that "To appreciate life, you must periodically defy death." After my flight, I'd say I'm pretty appreciative!

29

Once More with Feeling
Contact, Vol. II

The concept of contact and what it needs to feel like often mystifies lower level riders. They feel the reins in their hands but they don't maintain a consistent feel of the horse's mouth.

I sometimes tell them the story of the little girl I met who lived in the suburbs and always wanted a horse even though her parents couldn't afford one.

This girl was a dreamer and a bit of a fanatic. She would ride her bike around the neighborhood sitting on the rear luggage rack to make the handlebars be farther away from her hands. Then she would attach short lengths of clothesline to the handlebars and hold them like reins as she pedaled.

This little girl understood how the two reins work in concert with one another. If she drew back on the left rein and didn't follow forward with the right one, she couldn't make the bike turn. If she drew back on the left and didn't maintain contact on the "outside," the handlebars would spin all the way to the left, lock, and she'd fall over. A good reason to figure out not to drop the outside contact!

Janet McCune from Brooksville, Florida, and her husband conduct unmounted seminars to help riders learn the feelings they need to master. One interesting exercise pairs up participants as "rider" and "horse." The "horse" is blindfolded and wears a riding helmet to which is attached a pair of "reins" (strings) at the sides of the chin harness. The "rider" holds the reins and walks behind steering her partner on a chosen course. If the contact isn't maintained on both reins, it becomes immediately obvious how confusing the directions are to the person being "ridden."

Many riders who've had the idea drilled into them of "riding back to front" and never pulling on the horse's mouth are afraid to do anything with their hands. For them I have to stress that Lightness is an important goal but it doesn't always derive from *being* light.

I point out that they must think of two distinct continua that describe their relationship with the bit. They are: Heavy versus Light and Hard versus Soft. Hard hands are bad. This doesn't preclude intentional moments of "non-allowing," but hard hands always produce a hard or defensive horse. On the continuum between Hard and Soft, good riders are always near the Soft end of the spectrum.

Heaviness is certainly not a goal, but tactically there are times when getting in the horse's way enough to cause him to re-think the relationship is the way to proceed towards lightness. Realize that it is possible and occasionally necessary to be both Soft and Heavy at the same time to get this message across.

I am impatient with the devotees of Dressage *Lite*. These are the people who are so ideologically bound to the concept of Lightness that they will pursue it to the exclusion of any meaningful change happening in their horses. An old friend and teacher of mine, Colonel Aage Sommer, always used to remind us that "Things Take Time." It's true!

But on the other hand I'm reminded of the man who had fallen upon financial hard times. Every Wednesday and Saturday before the MegaMillions drawing he would pray to God to win the lottery and shed his burden. Finally one afternoon as he knelt in humble supplication, he heard a deep voice that resonated from the roiling clouds above, "BUY A TICKET!"

Back in 1981, the first year I met Major Lindgren, his English was still fairly primitive. I wrote down these exact words of his, "Many times in life God will help you, but in riding, not so very much. In riding you've got to help yourself!"

I need to add one disclaimer here because I'm not meaning to advocate force or strength other than that time-proven cliche that counsels your aids to be "as little as possible, as much as is necessary."

My wife long ago was riding in a clinic conducted by a "short list" quality teacher. The clinician was married to a prominent international trainer about whom she told this story. Her husband used to coach her, and with one particular horse, he kept saying, "Hold him and push. Hold him and push till he gives."

"Well, I did that for ten years," she said, "and the horse never gave. Not till I softened first and *then* he gave to me." I try never to forget this. All training is a combination of "making" and "allowing." It's easy to get mired in an ego thing that tips too close to the "Make him do it" end of the spectrum.

Conspiring to make him think he *wants* to do it, which often includes making the first offer, is a far more satisfying approach.

30

Dressage-Enabled
by the Y Chromosome and a Good Suntan

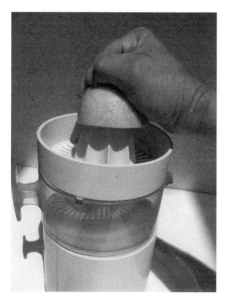

I've noticed that riders with certain demographics bring special skills to their lessons. For instance, Floridians are often better able than most other riders to keep their horses' polls supple.

I believe this is directly attributable to their practice of making fresh-squeezed orange juice. If every morning you pull out that little strainer with the upright knurl in the middle and work half oranges around on it till all the juice and tissue is removed, you gain the sense of how pliable and maneuverable your horse's poll should be. This isn't a crude see-sawing—those Dollar Store juicers are pretty fragile, you know. It isn't that his head should be moving all the time. It's that you have to maintain in him the ability to re-position and move it easily and at your will.

I also have a theory as to why men have an easier time with dressage than do women. It's because of how we practice with the TV remote. It has been said that men aren't interested in watching television. We are interested in watching what *might be* on television. We can see two seconds of Leno, two seconds of Letterman, two seconds of "NightLine," "CSI," "SportsCenter," "Animal Planet," and so on in endless

71

rotation and have some semblance of an idea of what's happening on each. Men are not hindered, as women are, by having an attention span.

In dressage this can work to our advantage. To get bogged down and overly focused on any particular aspect of what your horse is doing is disadvantageous. It doesn't mean you shouldn't notice, it just means that you have to ride the whole horse the whole time.

A specific skill that pilots learn is a ritualized scan of the instrument panel which they do about every 30 seconds and in exactly the same way each time. They don't get stuck on any one instrument or what it means nor do they overlook any of the others. This, whether you are man, woman, or otherwise is a useful technique to cultivate. Maintain an overview of your horse's behavior and training. Don't get sucked into any one problem or response and miss the big picture.

31

Coming Distractions
Nobody Said It Was Easy

Competitors rightfully want conditions to be perfect when they go out to show. I remember seeing Isabel Werth absolutely silence the crowd with a baleful glare right before she entered the ring at Aachen. But real life intrudes and situations beyond everyone's control must be dealt with.

There's the story of the show in Connecticut back in the '70s where the rides continued on despite a house across the street burning to the ground. A friend who rode hunters as a kid told me of riding an outside course over fences in the infield of a New Hampshire racetrack while a demolition derby took place around the outside. There's the tale of the hot air balloon ascension, the roaring sphere popping up over the trees during a Pan Am selection trials at Gladstone 30-some years ago.

But there are better ones. I was teaching a very nice older lady on a little white Arabian, getting her ready for her recognized show debut to be held at

the Tampa Fairgrounds. This was her last lesson on the Wednesday before the weekend show and she'd just received her ride times.

"I'm not riding," she announced.

"Why not?" I asked and encouraged, "He's being fine, and all you have to do is ride him the same way you do at home."

"I can't. My ride is at 10:30."

"Sooo?" I said, obviously missing the point.

"That's when the car drop is scheduled!"

I came to discover that the show management had contracted for the "horse show grounds" portion of the fair-grounds, but that another group was holding their function directly adjacent. This was Z-93, THE POWER PIG, a local metalhead rock station.

"Be the ninety-third caller and you can win a spot on our grid. Come to the fairgrounds on Saturday and if the Z-93 chopper drops our wreck on your square, you'll win a new Mazda!"

So picture a thousand shrieking fans, blaring music, whirling rotorblades, and my little lady on her Arab.

I am happy to report that I did talk her into doing it anyway, and she managed a 60%. I wasn't able to watch her ride in person. I chose the car drop instead and was able to video that entire proceeding. I was a bit disappointed because they'd taken all the good stuff out of it. No fiery eruption from the gas tank. Just a big splat like having pushed a fat pumpkin off a window ledge. Oh, and they missed the grid entirely on the first drop, had to pick up what was left of the car, and drop it again. It wasn't like dressage where you only get one chance!

Not renting all you thought you had has gotten organizers into trouble before. "Way Back When" Jane Savoie, Janet Black, and I were conducting a precursor to the USDF Adult Camps for a group in northern Vermont. The format was five days of lessons and lectures followed by a show on the weekend. The venue was a fairgrounds in Essex Junction that featured a harness track. The three dressage arenas were set up in the infield of the track.

All was going well until Tuesday when a procession of tractor trailers drove onto the grounds. A traveling circus had come to town, and it had rented the other half of the infield as well as the track's grandstand in front of which they would hold their performances.

What ensued was a little distracting to the clinic participants. The horses were mightily aware of the bellows and roars of the elephants and the lions. That "predator smell" was in the air. Then there were the visual distractions.... a woman high on a tower practicing twirling around on a rope held in her teeth.... three bears in turquoise leisure suits parading by on unicycles.

Saturday's show would coincide with an actual performance of the circus; so the organizers had wisely moved the arenas out of the infield and as far away on the backstretch as they could get them. This wasn't quite far enough. That afternoon Carol Lavell had an FEI ride at 3:30 and had to compete for her horse's attention with the Human Cannonball act.

Moral: Remember Carol and don't complain if someone snaps a photo or puts his quarters in the Coke machine during your ride some day!

32

Reach Out and Touch
But Not Too Much

I try to reinforce the notion of self-carriage, what it feels like, and how to avoid the common pitfalls of attempting to collect your horse that will prevent you from achieving it. Avoiding the "grab and hold till he gives" scenario is all important. It's more about surrounding your horse with the influence of the aids than it is about physically supporting him.

Nancy Golden

Two examples:

Looking for that "surrounding" feeling? Throw pots! No, not at your spouse or your children. As the photo illustrates, making a bowl or a vase on a potter's wheel takes a delicate touch. Grab the spinning clay too firmly

and you'll have mud all over the room and your lap! Surround it, shape it, mold it between directing and receiving aids. Work on its perimeters and surfaces—limit its boundaries as it revolves rather than crushing it together with your strength and you just might create a piece of art.

Another useful image allows me to tell you about the only musical instrument that you play without ever actually touching it. This is a device named for its inventor, an exotic character from the early part of the last century named Leon Theremin. Theremin was a scientist, inventor, and part-time Russian spy living in the U.S. during the

Stalin years. His work in electronics in the 'teens contributed to the invention of television. The instrument looked like a small wooden box with a pair of antennae, one straight and one looped. The circuitry produced an electromagnetic field around the antennae. So, to "play" the Theremin, you learned to disrupt the field by moving your hands through it. This changed the pitch of the sound that came out and made notes.

Again, it's not 100 percent analogous because you do, indeed, "touch" the horse both with the contact of your seat, legs, and hands, and with the pressures of the aids. But the idea of influentially surrounding the horse rather than imprisoning him in a vise-like grip is much more like the way a Theremin is played.

Two minor notes of interest: In speaking with my Dad about this story, he revealed he was not only familiar with the Theremin but saw L.T. play his invention in person in Philadelphia in 1934.

And even if you have never seen a Theremin, you have heard one being played. The Beach Boys used one in their electronically ground-breaking song, *Good Vibrations*. The Theremin also produced all those spooky, warbling electronic sounds that kept you up all night after watching 1950s grade B science fiction flicks on late night TV.

33
Film at Eleven
Which Is Reel and Which Is An Illusion?

I bought myself a movie camera in the early 1970s, the kind that let you pay three or four dollars to take three minutes and 20 seconds of scratchy footage (50 feet of film) and then pay a few more dollars and wait a week for it to come back from the developer. Primitive though the technology was, it let us look at ourselves critically and also allowed us to record riding events of note.

I used to splice together chunks of film into narratable stories and show them to my students at "movie nights" we'd arrange every so often. At big events like the '76 Olympics and the '78 Eventing World Championships, I'd come home with dozens of those little spools of film and spend hours rearranging and glueing them into some meaningful order.

When videotape arrived on the scene, I was more than ready. At the time I was teaching a teenage girl whose mother was an innovative thinker and one who was willing to put her cash on the line to prove her point. This was the early 1980s, and about the only commercial dressage-related videos that existed were a set by Bruce Davidson that consisted mostly of him sitting astride, speaking extemporaneously about some point (seemingly endlessly) and then going off to demonstrate it.

My student's mom was Judy Noone (also mother of the then 10-year-old but now well known international competitor and trainer, Tom Noone.) Judy along with a friend wanted to make a whole library of topic-oriented educational dressage videos and founded a company called Learning Partners. She planned to recruit a whole group of professionals to take the various tapes, but since I was teaching Laura, her daughter, she gave me first dibs on the topics I wanted to do.

On the list were subjects such as Flying Changes and Canter Pirouettes, but it seemed to me that most riders working on those movements probably already had a trainer and weren't too likely to be buying training tapes. On the other hand, everybody wanted to know about *Putting Your Horse On the Bit* and almost everybody needed to learn about *Leg Yielding*; so those were the topics I chose to do.

As an aside I might mention that these were the right choices. For a full 20 years I received royalty checks every January, and while that wasn't the reason I had gotten involved, they were a pleasant result of the work.

My approach to the videos was really pretty common, but it hadn't been applied to dressage topics before. Start with a natural sounding, readable script. Make up story boards with specific shots of specific durations to illustrate the text. Arrange a shooting script to get the shots in an order of convenience for the trainer (me) and the film crew. Devise graphics. Go in the studio to do standups for intros and lead-ins. Record the voiceover narrative. Take the VHS windowdubs home. (These were VCR-compatible copies of all the multiple takes of all the raw footage with a running, superimposed, on-screen time code to let me identify each piece I wanted to use.) Then create a long list of

"In/Out" times to help the editor place all the brief segments in order. Finally, go back into the studio to put it all together. Nowadays you could do most of that at home quite easily with a Mac or a PC, but then it was pretty exotic and loads of fun.

One side benefit of my forays into the world of video was that people would buy or rent them and would often have heard my voice long before they ever actually rode with me in a clinic or workshop.

One auditor in Utah approached me and said, "You know, I have your tapes and every morning I get up at 5:30, go downstairs to the rec room, put your video on, and watch it while I exercise on my stationary bike. Now that you're here in person, and I'm sitting listening to you, it just makes me want to pedal!"

34
Video Adventures, Vol. 2
Making "Introductions"

In the early '80s, I began to travel and teach, and gained some visibility through my participation at the National Instructors Seminars at Violet Hopkins's farm in Michigan. There I met Lowell Boomer who was President and Executive Director of USDF. It was his wont to float ideas around the dressage community to gauge how they'd be received by a larger audience. After the '84 Seminar, he sent me an outline of material to be covered in some proposed Instructor Workshops he hoped to institute. I responded favorably and added a few suggestions, one of which was that since Workshop Leaders would be going where dressage wasn't always "spoken" that it might be well to equip them with some visual aids to take along. I sent him a copy of the two Learning Partners videos, not that they themselves should be used, but to indicate what kind of stuff I was talking about.

It wasn't long after that that Lowell approached me with another idea. Many groups—some GMOs, but more often 4-H or horse clubs of every description—would call the USDF office seeking to rent a dressage video to show at their meeting. At that time the office had nothing to offer them; so it was decided to produce or acquire something that the USDF could stand behind when they handed it out. A production company had been contacted; Farnam would be the sponsor. Would I head this project for USDF?

My reaction, of course, was "Oh, boy! More playthings! Why not?"

This production needed to be bigger than "me," and while I would do the writing and editing, someone of greater national prominence would be the featured rider. My biggest worry was that I would be saddled with an Ego who would want to rewrite everything, and that we'd spend all our time bickering over whose path to follow. My final choice, approved by the USDF, couldn't have worked out better. I already knew Kathy Connelly: she had helped me with my horse, and she had been seen succeeding in national competition at the old Insilco Championships that drew people to Kansas City in those days. I have to say Kathy was perfect.

Filling the role of the jetsetting young professional that I was pretending to be, I hopped a plane and zipped down to Philly for a quick airport meeting with the Houston-based production company. Its head, Darolyn Butler, seemed quite surprised that I had a plan and seemed to know what I was doing. Their earlier videos, which featured famous reiners, calf ropers, and barrel racers, led her to expect to lead the clueless-in-the-ways-of-video "talent" through the exercise by the hand.

Our plan followed roughly the same lines as the Learning Partners one had with a few extra stops along the way for review and oversight in the person of Lazelle Knocke, S judge and a later USDF President. The Texas crew shot this one on 1" tape that was so-called "broadcast quality" in that era. Using window-dubbed VHS copies of the raw footage, I compiled edit lists and took them to Houston for the first of two four-day, near-round-the-clock studio sessions. Working with 1" tape required heavier duty equipment than they themselves owned, so they rented time in a big commercial house owned by a guy named Bill Young.

I never met Young in person but I was familiar with him. He'd made a mint back then recording a series of AM radio ad spots for the drag racing circuit. All those times you heard a radio anywhere in the country shouting "SUUUUNNNNDAAAAYYYYY, Don't miss wheel standing funny car action at...," that was Bill Young's doing. He went on to make major investments in the recording industry and had a keen eye for talent. At one point we were perusing his library for suitable background audio and discovered artifacts on the wall like the group *Boston*'s first platinum album, a check for a million bucks, and a framed handwritten note that simply said, "To Bill Young, Without you 'Lucille' would still just be a country girl, [signed] Kenny."

The studio was plush. The editor used to work for Walter Cronkite, and his fingers flew over the edit board the way they had when he'd been on a 15-minute deadline before the CBS Evening News went on air.

In the studio across the hall another crew was putting together a *Foreigner* rock video. I peered in through the glass at them, noticing an especially attractive young blonde woman who seemed to be in a position of authority, and thinking that their project was immensely more fascinating than my own. A few moments later, the young lady in question tapped on our window and cracked the door open. "Is this a DRESSAGE video?" she wondered aloud, adding, "My name is Patti. I have a Hanoverian!"

While putting our program together, we ran into unanticipated obstacles, each to be dealt with one way or another. For instance, I had planned to use 90 seconds of Kathy's Intermediaire Freestyle ride from Kansas City as the picture backdrop for some introductory voiceover I'd written. Her ride had been performed to the theme from *Chariots of Fire*. We contacted the composer to seek his permission and ascertained that Warner Brothers held the rights to it. A check with them determined that, yes, we could use the music, but it would cost us $50,000 for the privilege! Instead I rummaged around in the used record bins in a shop in Harvard Square and found a perfectly nice vinyl of Strauss waltzes for 50 cents. This we back-timed and over-dubbed right up to the actual applause after Kathy's performance, and no one was any the wiser.

The text also called for a "bad example" rider, and I had enlisted a good sport middle-aged student to fill that role. During the in-arena taping sessions, I'd shout, "No, Connie, NOT BAD ENOUGH! Do it again. Stiffer! Bounce more!" and she would dutifully try to comply. At one point we needed a shot of her making a very crooked canter, and she just couldn't get her horse's haunches in far enough. The solution was to shoot her face on coming around the corner to turn down the centerline. Then we cut, put Kathy on Connie's horse, shot her from the boots-down only, and let her ride a sort of travers. When we edited it as a match-action, no one could tell it wasn't a continuous flow of the original rider.

When we were putting the video together in the Houston studio, the producer decided we needed another voice to introduce me on the tape. She had just the guy she said, someone she used all the time. Could I audition him on the phone and see if he'd do? she asked.

Darolyn made the introductions and asked him to read a little paragraph and handed me the phone. What followed was a mellifluous baritone Johnny Cash "aah shucks, pardner" kind of reading that probably worked just fine for a barrel racing tape but didn't fit in with the Brandenburg Concerto background music or me. Darolyn and I held a brief whispered conference. She took the phone and instructed him, "Try it with a lot less hambone," and gave the receiver back to me. He then re-read me the same paragraph in a voice that sounded amazingly like Peter Jennings reporting from Vienna. Problem solved!

Our finished video became *The Official USDF Introduction to Dressage,* and it circulated widely for a number of years, not only in feed stores and tack shops but in some regular video rental outlets and public libraries.

Some time later I was on a plane to Central America to judge and found myself sitting beside a woman who was joining her husband and some friends on a surfing expedition to Costa Rica's Pacific beaches. We traded "What do you do" small talk. Upon my mention that I did horses, she told me her daughter was in a Pony Club north of Seattle. After a few more questions she admitted she recognized me from the USDF video they'd shown the kids. Small world!

Another time I had gone to Missoula, Montana, to do a clinic. I arrived a day early to let my hosts treat me to a tour of the National Bison Range up near Flathead Lake. It was the most beautiful spring morning you could imagine: bright blue sky, the gentle caress of a cool breeze, and a zillion wild flowers sparkling with dew. When we left the park around three in the afternoon, we were pretty starved and, by my estimation, in the middle of nowhere. On a deserted two lane highway we found a restaurant. The parking lot was empty, but the sign said "Open." We were sitting at a booth overlooking the snowcapped Mission Range and discussing plans for the next day's clinic, when the waitress interrupted, "Are you talking about DRESSAGE?"

Some chitchat revealed that not only was she trying to learn dressage on her horse, but she also owned our video!

35

Grin and Bear It
Where Minds Go When They're Uncomfortably Numb

The dressage professional up in northern Minnesota who hosted my clinics there hardly ever had to go to the store to buy red meat. Her husband was a hunter and once a year he took a few weeks off to stock their freezer with fresh game—venison, elk, antelope, and so on. It all seemed rather ordinary to them so when I came to spend the weekend, she would spring for something extra special for me—like chicken!

I made it known that I would really prefer to sample all their "normal" fare, after which the evening menus became far more exotic. As we sat down to dinner one evening when she was serving his bear steaks, her husband casually observed, "You know some people think that bear meat tastes a lot like human flesh."

"Wait a minute," I thought, "Just *who* exactly has tried both? Those Chilean soccer players, after all, weren't sampling bear I don't believe and...." Well, you see what I mean.

During the clinic lessons, one particular boy always hung around the barn. He rode a little bit at the farm but not with me. A lumpy kind of kid, his name wasn't Jerome but it could have been. He was the recipient of a good amount of teasing and flirtatious attention from the teenage girls who found him non-threatening, and he helped out by fussing over things and by preparing the lunches for everyone.

It was bitter cold that day, the kind of day when it takes a lot of extra energy just to get through it. As I taught I was bundled up in a horse blanket and sitting in front of a propane space heater. The "what bear tastes like"

"KELLIE"

story of the night before had just drifted through my mind when I overheard Jerome discussing what he planned to make for lunch later that day.

I said to him, "So Jerome, if you were going to cook yourself and serve you to us for lunch, how would you prepare yourself?"

He thought it over briefly, smiled, and announced he thought he'd make a nice pot roast. A good choice I agreed.

Things went rapidly downhill from there. As each subsequent rider came in for their lesson, the stalwart little group of frozen auditors and I discussed how each should be cooked and presented to best effect. Our attractive host(ess), we determined, would make a nice little standing crown roast, wild rice mounded in the center, steamed asparagus on the side. An ingenue home on spring break from college was slated to become cutlets, sautéed in butter and white wine. A well-worn lady of considerable age and experience we whispered might best be made into jerky.

"But what would you be?" they all wanted to know.

"Only the best," I answered. "I want to be served as haggis."

36
Dance with the Girl That Brung Ya

As a judge, I'm always grateful when riders appear to heed my advice. If someone is blasting around in her first test on Saturday, running her horse off his feet and out of rhythm, it's disappointing if she does the same thing in front of me all weekend long. The same thing goes for very long reins, for circles that miss their marks or have corners, for leg yieldings done with the outside leg braced out in space, and a variety of other, easily correctable mistakes.

As a coach, however, my reaction to some judge's advice is "Well, yes, but we can't solve that today. Keep doing what you're doing, don't worry about it, and we'll get it fixed over the next six months."

Then there's "advice" best left ungiven. An inexperienced student of mine rides a fairly tense Arabian with whom she has a somewhat tenuous relationship. She went off on her own to a show to ride several Training Level tests. The first one was quite acceptable under the circumstances, scoring in the low 60s. Below the Collectives the judge wrote "You need to use your seat more." Trying to please, my student did just that, got her horse totally inverted by driving it around inexpertly, and came back with a 54 percent.

Talking about it at her next lesson, I explained that I thought her judge had made a bad choice of words while trying to be helpful. I agreed with what she probably meant to say in that as her seat becomes more sophisticated, it will be more helpful in conducting the horse's rhythm and in balancing the canter. But MORE doesn't equate to BETTER, and this was a case where she'd have been better off filing that advice away and learning to apply it over a much longer time frame than in a crash course between rides.

When TV sports guys interview some old coach about switching quarterbacks during the playoffs, the coach always squints, (most likely) spits, and delivers some homily about how his pappy always told him, when you go to a social, ya gotta dance with the girl that brung ya. The same thing applies here.

You Gotta Have Heart
And a Certain Amount of Chutzpah

A clinic rider expressed to me her insecurities about trying to train her own horse. She worried that she didn't sit well enough, that her aids weren't clever enough, that she couldn't make the best decisions to help her horse.

In general, these are all legitimate concerns and I applauded her for being empathetic enough to care. At the same time I said to her (and she was by no means a helpless, uncoordinated novice without a seat), "If you found yourself on a desert island with no shelter, you'd find a rock, a stick, a shell, and a coconut husk, and you'd manufacture your own tools. With them you'd make some sort of hut even if you didn't have your Craftsman lock wrenches or your power auger with you."

If you school your horse by yourself, that's the kind of attitude you need to have towards your work. Yes, you must always strive to improve your "tools," but in the meantime it's better to do *something* with the tools you do have than to back off into passive self-paralysis, riding conservatively and accomplishing nothing. As your tools improve, your goals will be easier to attain, but "making do" with what you've got is the only practical way to approach your training until that day arrives.

Riders who are crude, lack self awareness, or can't contain their emotions aren't the people I'm speaking to here. But most other riders can go out on some short limbs, try some creative solutions, and safely back out of them if the right results aren't forthcoming. I'm always struck by how patient and forgiving most horses are with us as we muddle along. When we finally figure it out, they're probably more relieved than we are, but in the meantime they tolerate all the "trying" better than you might imagine.

Practically Speaking
Capt. Jack Sparrow: "They're not rules, they're *guidelines.*"

Don't get me wrong. I think dressage writing is valuable, particularly when it helps you crystallize in your mind a concept whose feeling you've brushed up against in your actual riding experience. I am less enthralled with those articles that use up seven pages of text accompanied by glossy photos and elaborate, arrowed diagrams of hoof patterns just to describe a canter depart. It's not that the information is untrue. I just don't think it's all that relevant to discovering how to make one correctly.

I also find it tedious to read theory so detached from reality that it makes me wonder if the author remembers what it's like to ride a normal horse. It's unfortunate that often by the time someone is of sufficient stature to be published, they are a) old and forgetful, or b) no longer having to put up with the kind of horses that their readers have to cope with.

In the previous vignette (above this one) one reason the woman felt so timid about schooling her horses was that they didn't feel like the descriptions of correctly trained ones she found in the literature.

One true expert whom I knew and rode with a little bit back in the '70s was Dr. H.L.M van Schaik. He was a feisty old Dutchman and a veteran of the 1932 Olympics. He was unabashedly grounded outside my (and most people's) reality, didn't care one bit, and freely admitted it. As he said, he was interested in *classical* dressage. To practice it, you needed a baroque-type horse with a natural willingness to collect and you needed an appropriate venue, predictable and free of distractions to allow you to gain the horse's trust and to train along van Schaik's classical principles. That what he was preaching wouldn't work on a three-year-old Thoroughbred out in a big field on a windy day wasn't his problem. He didn't even think it was supposed to apply to those situations.

I am much more of a pragmatist. I've had the good fortune to be influenced by some of the last generation of real cavalrymen, in particular Colonel Aage

Sommer (DEN), Colonel Bengt Ljungquist (SWE), and most especially Major Anders Lindgren (SWE). They all lived and worked in the "real world" with horses.

Back in the early '80s, I was watching Colonel Sommer teaching at the National Instructors Seminar. A horse was very stuck in his shoulders and wouldn't turn on the haunches at all. In my wide-eyed naiveté I was thinking of the right recipe to apply when Colonel Sommer told the rider to take her outside leg up onto the shoulder in front of the saddle and give him a couple of good "boots" till he moved over. "You can do that?" I thought. The idea of breaking out of the standard mold and doing whatever the horse needed was new to me as was the idea that during a movement the aids could be fluid and your leg didn't have to stay in the same place the whole time.

On another occasion a horse was unwilling to leg yield. The rules and the recipe, of course, demand a straight horse, positioned only at the poll. Colonel Sommers's advice: "Open the inside rein; overbend him; let him fall over his outside shoulder, and just get him moving sideways. When he'll yield at all, then you can make him straight."

These examples might not strike you as "classical," but in both cases the horse's "light went on," and his education was able to proceed from there. And isn't that what it's all about?

39

Unclassically Correct

A good rule of thumb is "If your horse is willing to do something, don't practice it to death. Work on what he won't do." If he wants to be slow, make him fast. If he wants to be short, make him long. Be sure your horse is versatile and adjustable because if you aren't aware, he can easily take something that in principle is desirable and turn it into an evasion.

I see novice riders who slavishly work to make their horses round but don't realize when roundness has become leaning and leaning has become rigidity. It happens in all the gaits, but it's especially prevalent in the canter where you see horses barreling around with their riders half-standing in the irons and looking like they're waterskiing along behind them.

Dressage people are fond of the quote about our discipline being the foundation of all other kinds of training, and in one respect that's quite true. At the same time, I am highly suspicious of horses that are schooled in a way that they can *only* go in a frame. Before you ride him on the bit all the time, your horse ought to be broke enough and balanced enough to simply go around like a civilized creature. And even an upper level horse should still be able to hack long and free like a pleasure horse without running off or falling on his face.

Just the other day I encountered another horse who had no sense of natural self-carriage under saddle. In the canter, although he was flexed, he was strong, heavy, deep, and on the forehand. My prescription to his rider was "Ride him above the bit!" Even if she had to haul him up there at first, it was better to get him off her hands. Then she could slow him down and stabilize his tempo so if she gave, he would stay the same. From there she could make him round again without him taking advantage, and then her half halts could shift his weight to the rear.

"Make him put his head up in the air," doesn't sound like very conventional dressage-like advice, but in this case it paved the way to a relationship that wasn't unreasonably slanted in the horse's favor.

40

The Russians Are Coming! The Russians Are Coming!

Every now and then I am party to an especially memorable lesson. Sometimes it's a really good one; sometimes it's a spectacular disaster. Here's one that I think you'll agree wasn't routine.

I used to teach kids—a zillion of them—when I was young. I don't much anymore, but at a clinic up in the Florida Panhandle, my past returned. The night before, the organizer asked me if I minded doing one semi-private lesson. "It's a pair of brothers," she explained. "They're adopted. Their mom went to Russia to bring home one, found there were two, and brought them both back. They're really nice!"

"No problem," I said, little realizing.

Turns out the brothers, Alex and Andrew, were seven and nine years old and mounted on a pair of Merrylegs-type ponies, each with a mind of its own. One pony was a little ball of fire that careened around the ring; the other would barely move. The boys, as advertised, were very cute—all blond hair and smiles. I would ask them a question. A brief exchange in Russian would follow, and then would come a cheerful answer.

The lesson was chaotic. I'd get them going around the arena, but the lazy one would stop dead on the track. Then the second pony would crash into him fullspeed, and the boys would erupt into uproarious laughter. I tried setting up sets of cones to give them some focus. A circle didn't work. I tried a slalom. Nope. I tried pole bending. Unsuccessful. I glanced at my watch. I'd only used up 11 minutes of the hour. All the while I was thinking, "Oh, dear, their mother is *paying* for this. Paying a lot!"

Semi-at wit's end, I grabbed a plastic bottle of water and introduced them to the "spit take." This is a comedic device you've probably seen on Seinfeld or in an old Mel Brooks movie. I remember seeing Carl Reiner give an elaborate demonstration on an old Johnny Carson show. It happens when in the middle of a sip of water someone startles you with a shocking or outrageous comment and you accidentally spray a misty cloud all over the place.

With a little practice the boys became quite accomplished. "Now," I suggested to them, "ride around and see how wet you can get your brother."

Suddenly they were transformed. Alex got very quick with the whip and his lazy pony popped into life. Andrew's pony found that running off was no longer a viable option. The kids rode like crazy and exceedingly well. By the end they were soaked but happy. And their Mom had videoed the whole proceedings—something to show to their wives in 20 years!

As we finished, I said to Andrew, "So answer me one question. How does it feel to be named after a hurricane?"

"Pretty good," he smiled.

Brother Alex interjected proudly, "And my middle name is Ivan!"

41

I Came, I "Seed," I Saw
And Look What Happened!

There aren't many things you can do in a dressage test that ramp up the judge's Cringe Factor more than to see-saw your horse's head down. It just drives us nuts. And it will often earn you a 4 for Rider Position and Correct Use of the Aids. A rider gets those hands going; the nose gets wig-wagging, and pretty soon, even if her hands get quiet, the nose just keeps waving back and forth.

Maybe you recall seeing that iconic old newsreel from the '40s of Galloping Gertie. Not a girl, not a horse, Galloping Gertie was a bridge and a vivid example of the destructive effects of harmonic resonance. This was back before engineers subjected bridge models to wind tunnel testing, and they accidentally built this huge bridge across the Tacoma Narrows in Washington State with too much wind resistance in the superstructure and not enough lateral bracing. When the wind caught the bridge just right, the whole roadway started first to sway and then to buck wildly as the wave motion kept reinforcing itself. The denouement featured the entire seven million dollar edifice ("edifice wrecks," one supposes) plunging into the water far below.

I always think of that nightmarish bridge scenario when I see riders sawing on their horses' mouths.

The worst part is that half the time the riders swear they aren't doing it. I had one regular clinic student out West whose hand behavior was so egregious that I wanted to call her "Tom's Sister." [Explanation below if needed]

"Why does his head go back and forth?" she'd ask.

"Because you're pulling it back and forth."

` "No, I'm not."

And so on. I would get on the horse and his head would be steady. She'd get back on and it would wave. I'd have her ride with the reins in one hand and his head would be steady. She'd take the reins normally, fall into her unconscious habit, and immediately it would wig-wag again. All the while she would deny that her hands moved, even if all the people at ringside would testify that her hands were at fault.

One day in anticipation of my trip to that farm and knowing I would see more of the same, I trekked to Office Depot and bought a selection of posterboards, glues, and markers. Then I constructed a full-sized replica of the yellow highway sign you see that means "Playground—Children at Play," put a big red circle with a diagonal hash mark over it, and carted it onto the airplane to present to her.

91

Unfortunately the receipt of my handiwork made the party in question angry enough that she decided not to speak to me for some months (can't win 'em all), but everyone did report that her hands got much better.

[From above: "Tom," of course referred to Tom _Saw_yer.]

42

Access Granted

Some riders seem to think that if they tell their horse something once, he should just remember it and that response should always be there waiting to replicate itself. It would suit everybody just fine if horses worked like that. They rarely do, of course. Keeping all the answers you might require from your horse available every minute you're on him is a chore, but it's at the core of educated, thoughtful riding.

If you're old enough, you may recall watching "The Ed Sullivan Show" on TV Sunday evenings back in the '50s and '60s. The program was a vaudeville montage of variety acts seemingly thrown together: a comedian, an Elvis Presley, a dancing troupe, the Beatles, Maria Callas, and so on. Aside from the high dollar acts that viewers tuned in for, Ed would intersperse odd assortments of Hungarian acrobats, talking dogs, and similar fare to fill the hour.

My favorite was always the guy who came out and spun plates on long sticks. The trick was to keep them all spinning at once—never to lose track and let one tumble off and crash to the ground.

It's this very same constant attention to every detail that you need to mimic to keep each muscle and nerve-ending in your horse tuned, primed, and ready for duty. If you coast around and forget to keep _his_ plates spinning all the time, you shouldn't be surprised if his reactions don't measure up to your expectations!

43
Bow? Wow!

Some people just can't stop themselves from teaching their horse tricks. It makes for some surprises if you don't know those tricks are programmed in.

I was teaching a teenager at a monthly Daytona clinic. The girl was new to me and likewise new to dressage. Her horse was a little gray Arabian (naturally) that was flat, lazy, and would only bend to the left. The rider was sweet but to call her passive would be to overstate her vigor.

I tried all the ways I could to get them together: transitions, spiral yieldings on the circle, but she was just never getting below the very surface of her horse's responses. Finally I said to her, "Just take the whip, don't hurt him, but try to make him feel a little excited."

No difference.

I commanded again, "Go ahead and wake him up. Just get *any* response!"

"I don't understand," she whispered in reply.

"Come on over here for a second," I said, taking the whip from her. Then holding the rein in my left hand, I rather politely whacked him on his flank several times to ask him to move over. The next thing I knew and much to my astonishment, he went right to his knees and flopped down with his hindlegs underneath him, me still holding the rein.

"Aarrgh! Get up!" I exclaimed aghast and tapped him again, which only confirmed his intention to stay on the ground.

The girl smiled benevolently up at me, still astride him, and just said, "Oh, that's a trick I taught him." Eventually he regained his feet, and my next query was "And are there any *other* tricks I need to know about?"

I ran into another horse with a similar trick, but at least this time the owner warned me in advance. This horse was an older Andalusian, and he knew his trick so well that he would offer it at any gait. You could be cantering along and if you got your inside leg a little forward onto that button, look out! Down he'd go in a skidding bow quick as a flash. The question then was what to do next. Major Lindgren usually counseled, "When in doubt, yield them somewhere." I figured, "Well, the worst that can happen is he'll fall over, and he's so close to the ground already, it can't possibly hurt, so why not?"

It turned out that the horse was eager enough not to tip over completely that the leg yielding got him back up, moving, and back on the aids.

A much more public bow occurred years ago at an early Judges Forum at the American Dressage Institute. One of the FEI school horses, The Dutchman, was being used as a demo horse, and as his volunteer rider who'd been recruited to do a test halted at X to salute, he also lay right down with her. No one had explained his circus background to her, and that he knew not only to fling himself down, but to expect large cats to leap over him while lying there.

44

Dressage Grammar Spoken Here

I once had the fortune, good or otherwise, to teach the Western Pleasure Champion of Rhode Island who had decided she wanted some dressage lessons. In the course of her first ride I asked her what she used for canter aids. "Oh, nothing really," she said. "He just canters when he hears the announcer ask for it."

That's an extreme example, but riders from other disciplines use the words "aids," "cues," and "signals" more or less interchangeably. We dressage geeks are much more particular. To us, a cue or a signal elicits an entire behavior, like pushing the canter button for instance. You can think of a "cue" as being like a transitive verb. You give a bump with a leg, for instance, and the message is simple: "do THIS."

On the other hand, in dressage we like to say our "aids" are like a nonverbal language that we use to communicate with our horse. We use the aids in combinations. Individual "words" can be put together to produce more complex responses. Our aids are partly verbs, but they also function as adjectives and adverbs. These modifiers tell the horse not only what to do but *in what manner to do it*. So in dressage we're specifically not looking for a generic sort of reaction. Rather, being able to combine "the aids" in a myriad of ways lets us deal in the subtleties and nuances that shade the behavior we end up with.

This special infinitely-modifiable relationship we seek to create explains another phenomenon, namely where we say the horse sometimes "finishes the sentence for us"—not a good thing. Maybe that's just a fancy way to say he anticipates, but in this context it's like he's guessing how the modifiers are going to play on out.

It's bad enough when he guesses right. A friend of mine rode the Prix St. George on her old and very savvy Thoroughbred. I picked up her test sheet and ribbon later and was reading the judge's comments as I arrived back at their stall.

"You got a 9 for the halt/rein-back," I announced.

"I never asked him for that," Samantha responded quietly. "He just made up the whole thing himself."

Unfortunately, even if the result looked fine to the watchers, that amounted to a kind of rebellion, albeit a whimsical one, that we can't allow our horses to indulge in. Worse is when they finish our sentence a *different* way than we were planning to. Making your horse wait to hear the rest of your version of what's to happen next (and how) is a personal Valhalla that the rider of every smarter-than-us dressage horse is trying to reach.

45

Now Ladies and Gennelmen, a Little Champagne Music
(Spillwine Edition)

It's a long-held tradition in the foxhunting fraternity that if you "dismount without the permission of the Master," you owe the hunt a bottle of champagne. These are accumulated over the course of the hunting season and opened for the benefit of all at the annual Spillwine Dinner celebrating the season's end.

Long ago I instituted a similar policy for my lesson students. The idea is simple: fall off once in a lesson and that costs a bottle of champagne—domestic but not that awful Andre soda pop stuff. Second fall in the same lesson and the tithe becomes "imported." The third fall and it's a bottle of Dom. I always add, "And if I fall off in your lesson, I'll buy you a case of champagne."

Before I made up the rules, I had one embarrassing lesson wherein I, the teacher, managed to part company not once but TWICE from the same horse. The occasion was an after-school group lesson back in the '70s. Four youngish teens were riding, attended by their four future soccer moms (SUVs hadn't been invented yet). One of the horses, a hot little chestnut Quarter Horse mare, was being particularly contrary. She was all of 15.2 and cat-like in her movements. I climbed into the girl's tiny Stubben Rex to help out and immediately discovered that my boots wouldn't fit into the irons. It didn't matter anyway; the leathers weren't long enough to do any good. I had been aboard the mare for what seemed like seconds doing my rendition of balance-on-the-top-of-the-flagpole when in a quick, tornadic frenzy, she landed me unceremoniously on the ground. I jumped to my feet, smiled reassuringly to the horrified mothers, and remounted. Less than 30 seconds later in an instant replay of the first episode, she ditched me again. I did get back on, but it takes more nonchalance than I could muster to appear blasé after two disasters in such a short time.

A teenaged pupil of mine once did me one better than my double swan dive. She was (coincidentally?) riding another chestnut mare, this one a New Forest Pony, and again her size and quickness made staying glued on problematic. In the span of a single lesson, the pony "got" her three times and each time stood over her like "so what are you doing down there exactly?"

All this prompted the Champagne Rule, and it has served me well over the years. I collect a nice bottle every now and then. If the larder is bare, I have my students spend more time without their stirrups until the shelf fills back up.

I can recall a time when my rule came back to haunt me. A student of mine and I were schooling a pair of her very green Trakehners in a large, sloping pasture. I was trying to get mine around a 30-meter circle. His intention was to take me to the barn. He compromised by getting his legs completely tangled up and tumbled over himself to the spongy turf. As he skidded along on his shoulder with me trying frantically to keep rolling out of his way, I heard his owner already shouting to me enthusiastically about the case of champagne awaiting her.

46

Living in the Past
(The Future Hasn't Happened Yet)

Twenty-five years ago a student of mine acquired a fairly nice Grand Prix horse from Germany. This was a few years before the European pipeline for amateur advanced schoolmasters really opened up. At that time, although I had ridden all the GP movements on some assorted horses under supervision, I was struggling along with my self-made Thoroughbred St. George horse.

When I played around with the new horse, I made an interesting discovery. Standing at X, if I did one thing with my hips, I got piaffe; a different tilt and I got passage; another variation and the trot resulted. That shouldn't seem too surprising to you. What got my attention was the realization that had I done any of those three things on my own horse, I would have gotten one single trot-like answer. Not knowing any better, I hadn't taught him to discriminate between those refinements of the aids.

Getting on a different horse, even if it doesn't know a lot more than your own, can be such a "Duh Moment." It's your chance to redefine the spectrum of all those qualities we seek when we ride. How soft can "Soft" be? How much swing can a back have? How prompt is "Prompt"? How through is "Through"? And it's not necessary to feel all of these differences on any single horse.

One January 1st, I decided to keep track that year of all the different horses I rode. They could be at seminars or clinics or lessons or trying one for somebody. My rule was that I couldn't get on just for the sake of adding them to the list. There had to be a legitimate reason. And if I rode the horse in February and then got on him again in October, it still only counted as one. That year I kept a tiny notepad, and each evening that the occasion warranted, I'd add another name or two. At year's end, my list totaled 236. Multiply that over as many years as I've been doing this (and even subtracting for repeats from year to year) and you get a whole mess of horses.

The result is most of the time when I get on a new horse, I can say I've ridden this one before. True, "he" was a different color then. In fact, he was probably a composite of a half dozen other horses each with some of the qualities of the new one. But that experience allows you to say, "Wait, I know this can feel better. I've felt it be better before."

Filling your mental hard disk with as many of these experiences as you can, lets you hold each movement you do, each response you get, up to the light to see if its as "good and pure and right" * as it ought to be.

* the words of Meatloaf from "Bat Out of Hell."

47

Turning Japanese
For the Sake of Knowledge

Finding the variety of riding experiences mentioned above can be a problem. I know many amateur riders, especially ones who keep their horses at home, who may go weeks or months at a time without sitting on any horse but their own.

As is often the case, one Saturday evening during a clinic I was giving, the whole little group met for dinner. The riders were all friends with one another, and I persuaded them to try the local Japanese restaurant with me. Dead fish was a bit beyond them, but they did sit happily at the grill table consuming quantities of hot sake and being entertained by the chef's antic performance. Over the course of dinner this business of knowing no other horse but their own came up.

"I can fix that," I offered, while pouring another round of sake. "Hand me a paper napkin." With that, we re-wrote the next day's clinic schedule that originally had been seven hour long private lessons. With a lot of tinkering, we turned it into a series of 40 minute semi-privates where everyone would

get to ride two horses they'd never been on. All the riders were quiet and competent enough that nobody's horse would be put at risk of discomfort or worry.

The next evening as they packed up and headed for home, there was universal agreement that they'd all had one of the best clinic experiences of their lives.

That clinic featured one extra bit of unplanned drama. To make the schedule come out right, the riders corralled one of their friends who had only come to audit to take a half hour lesson. Since she hadn't brought her own horse along, a borrowed one that she didn't know was volunteered for her use. We convened next day bright and early at eight A.M. on a crisp (for February in Ocala) morning.

As we got going, I noticed a multi-colored hot air balloon floating in the distance. As the lesson proceeded, the balloon seemed to drift neither left nor right but appeared to grow in size. Fate and the prevailing winds were directing it not only towards us but literally right down the centerline at an altitude not exceeding two hundred feet.

The spectators all wondered how the horse in the ring would react when the balloon finally overflew us. Turns out he was quite a prince and faithfully kept his trot throughout. I must say, though, that I'd never before seen a horse simultaneously trotting and crouching so low to the ground that his belly nearly rubbed the sand!

48
Wheels of Fire

Some horses are very "adult" with a multitude of coping skills. Nothing ruffles them. An exception for many in these modern times is carriages, wagons, sulkies, and other wheeled vehicles that today's horses just aren't familiar with. I don't mean that they have to put up with being hitched themselves. Some can't stand even seeing a cart drawn behind another horse.

We used to own a big Swedish horse who had that very phobia. Without enough forethought we had our working student enter him in some Second Level tests being held at a training facility for harness horses. The show was to be run far on the backside of the track, but we hadn't taken into account the renter of a nearby offtrack shedrow who arrived in harness needing to drive his pacer across our warm-up to get to the track. Courtney was just ready to go in, and I had dire visions of Dino careening down the median strip of Highway 17 imagining his wheeled pursuer. Consequently we stationed an "asssistant"—namely her mother—to stand by the warm-up arena's gate with a fistful of 20 dollar bills to bribe the drivers to wait till our kid's ride was over before they drove through.

Steve Waller

Another time I had gone cross-country schooling at Bradley Palmer State Park up on the north shore above Boston. The New England Hunter Trials had been held there the previous year, and it was still possible to school over some solid, inviting fences and get in a good gallop. I was peacefully going about this chore, cruising down a cinder bridle path when my horse and I noticed a loud array of jingles and creaks coming from around the corner. Trotting briskly towards us, we encountered an ornate carriage being pulled by four striking leopard Appaloosas. Prior to that moment I had seen many Roadrunner cartoons, but I had never seen a 16.2 Thoroughbred have a Wile E. Coyote Moment, leaping three feet high, eyes out on stalks, legs churning in midair before they even hit the ground. Exit "Stage Left."

I am relieved to report that it isn't only my own horses that suffer from this affliction. At one Dressage at Devon quite a few years ago, a PR person dreamed up the idea of bringing the formally-attired judges to their booths for the Saturday evening performance in horse-drawn carriages. They failed to realize the carriages' route would have to take them through the competitors' warm-up. In this case it was Exit Stage Left, Right, Center, and through the Orchestra Pit. Not too many of the FEI horses thought driving horses was a very good idea either.

49
Stop, Drop, and Roll
When a Dressage Rider Must Decide to Sink or Swim

Hey, you know I didn't just fall off the turnip truck yesterday. I've been doing this a long time. I've seen show rings that were more aqua-unfirma than terra-firma. Ones where you might expect to see a periscope or a dorsal fin. I've even judged (we're talking recognized shows) where the ring surface was completely covered with a blanket of snow (as would the windshield of the "judge's box" have been if the wipers and the defroster weren't going full blast).

But recently one of my students reached a new (pardon the expression) high watermark in her showing career. Ironically, a few hours before, my little cadre at the show had presciently alluded to this then unwritten story. Several of them knew they had already gained, through one sort of misbehavior or another, unwitting inclusion in these pages. A third member of the group joked that she felt left out and she'd just have to do something to catch up with them.

This was just her second recognized show with a young Lusitano. Training Test 4 went well, and she was rewarded with a score pleasantly into the 60s. Then the downpour began. Lightning. Thunder. Everything but the plague of locusts. When the show resumed after a long delay, the arena had been inundated, but the footing seemed safe enough. The warm-up had to be conducted in the driveway, but her horse responded well to the conditions and began First Level 1 with no problem.

Until the free walk. Then he took it upon himself to pause mid-diagonal, paw gleefully, and despite his rider's protestations, collapse camel-like to

Paul Pedersen and Action Snapshot Photography

Score this!!

his knees and fling himself onto his side in the muck. No one could quite remember this occurring before other than at summer camp in Wisconsin, so it became the talk of the show grounds and clearly worth mentioning here. I wish I could offer you more pictures, but the photographer along with everyone else was in such hysterics that history, alas, went largely unrecorded.

The question arises: just exactly how you score this sort of misadventure? Believe it or not, the USEF Rules (DR 122.7f) don't prohibit you and/or your horse from falling down (or playing in the mud). The score is supposed to reflect how the incident "affects the performance of the movement," which in this instance was "substantially" to say the least. The judge, however, eliminated her citing the rule about prolonged resistance. Had I been judging, I'd have given her a one for the movement, a 4 for Impulsion (Desire to Move Forward), and a 3 for Submission (Attention and Acceptance) in the Collectives, but I would have judged the rest of the test and let it count. In my mind the "Resistance" wasn't prolonged enough to toss him out. Once he got wallowing, in fact, he didn't seem to be resisting at all. He appeared to be quite relaxed and refreshed.

50
Candygram from the Colonel

Everyone who teaches can recall a few truly memorable situations they've been in—good and bad. I had one of these where I teetered on the brink of disaster before a last-second rescue. The occasion was the final National Instructors Seminar held at Vi Hopkins's Tristan Oaks Farm in Michigan in 1989. After that, the Seminar was going to move on to Lincoln, Nebraska near the USDF offices.

For years Maryal Barnett, who chaired the Hopkins Seminar Organizing Committee, and Vi herself, who had been the founder and guiding force behind the program, had always stood in the background as the actual event unfolded. In its last Michigan year, they asked to be among the Participating Instructors, and who could deny them? Two extra slots were added.

Much of the daily seminar syllabus involved practice teaching and discussion, but at the end of each day, the 12 "PI"'s rode, divided into three groups of four and taught by the staff, in this case Major Lindgren, Robert Dover, and me. One group included three fairly advanced rider/trainers and Vi, and I can only speculate why the Major and Robert were so willing to have me do that group.

Violet had learned dressage back in the 1940s, in large part from Pops Konyot, then the head horse trainer for the Ringling Brothers Circus (note: also the father of Alex Konyot and Dorita Konyot Humphries and grandfather to long-listed dressage rider Tina Konyot). By 1989, Vi was nearly 80 and hadn't taken a riding lesson from anyone for years.

And I must say that as a student, she was absolutely dreadful. She was off in her own world and totally out of the habit of doing anything other than what she chose to do next. The result was chaos. She'd stop in the middle of the track at random times or invent ring figures that imperiled her fellow riders and their horses. My arena by this time had drawn a crowd of about 100 spectators, interested in seeing how I might manage this conflagration. (I think the prevailing thought was "OK, Smart Guy, we've heard you critique everybody. Let's see you teach your way out of THIS!")

Semi at wit's end and needing a real Hail Mary, I stopped the lesson, and announced, "Vi, you have a phone call!"

"I do?" she asked in her flustered little-old-lady voice.

"Yes, Vi, it's from Colonel Podhajsky. He says to shorten your reins!"

"Oh, my!" she exclaimed.

As the lesson proceeded, more calls and telegrams kept arriving from the long-deceased head of the Spanish Riding School: "Vi, look up." "Vi, watch where you're going." "Vi, push him into your hand and don't let him lean on your inside leg." Amazingly, she got much better, and my imminent disgrace as a teacher was narrowly averted.

The following winter I got a Christmas card from Miss Hopkins. After wishing us the greetings of the season, she appended, "You know, Bill, I'm still getting those telegrams!"

51

Of Push-Ups and Roasted Onions

No, not the Victoria's Secret kind. Not the Gold's Gym kind. We're talking Good Humor man here.

I'm always looking for imagery that helps riders better understand the mechanisms of how to make their horses feel more correct. You've undoubtedly heard a teacher say your horse should react as though you're sitting astride a big water balloon. When you squeeze with your legs, it should feel as though the water rushes to the front of the balloon, in a sense filling the reins with volumes of energy (but not necessarily a lot of weight).

A second image is the "push-up," that ice cream thing on a stick that comes in a cardboard tube. You push from the bottom (the hindquarters) and ice cream emerges from the other end. Each time you push, you get a result out the front.

I personally am fond of another one. (Note that we're making your dressage visualizations seasonally adjustable.) Ever had an oven roast with pan-roasted potatoes and onions? Maybe it's just a guy thing, but my guilty pleasure is taking a whole roasted onion onto my plate and mashing it with my fork so it telescopes out layer by layer in satisfyingly diminishing rings. I can never

do this without thinking of how the driving aids make the horse reach out through his topline into the bridle.

Why are these images important? Because if this idea isn't in play, you don't have a horse that's really on the bit. There's a reason dressage people don't use the term "headset" (unless it's for an iPod). Your horse isn't supposed to pose in a *static* frame; he's supposed to reach dynamically and elastically into the bit. The long and low stretching movement in Training and First Level is meant to demonstrate this ability, but the concept should be equally alive in a horse that's being ridden correctly in collection. Round isn't enough. "Round and Reaching" is the ticket.

52

I Got My First Real Six String Bought It at the Five and Dime Played It Till My Fingers Bled

Was the summer of ninety-one.

After a run of 12 years, the National Instructors Seminar was winding down. The fledgling Certification program was ready to kick in. But there was no longer a unifying high profile, national-scale educational activity on the USDF drawing boards.

At the time I was still chairman of the USDF Instructor-Trainer Council, and one morning standing around in the aisle of Charlotte Trentelman's barn, Charlotte, Susan (Woods), and I cooked up the framework for a National Dressage Symposium to be held the following spring.

In part, we were looking to showcase the work of our teacher, Major Anders Lindgren, whose philosophy, methods, and personality we felt deserved to be presented on a larger stage than the Instructor program had been able to provide.

Back in the mid '80s, Lindgren had offered up two names—friends of his—whom he thought could contribute to the Hopkins Seminars. At the time they were turned down for being, well, too *Scandinavian*—not enough in the mainstream of big time international dressage. One was a Finnish woman named Kyra Kyrklund who was finally welcomed to the States by an adoring American audience ten years later. The other was a Swedish lawyer and trainer named Eric Lette, who subsequently became chairman of the FEI Dressage Committee. Anders, Eric, and I had conducted the National Instructors Seminar at the University of Nebraska in 1990, and I knew Eric and Major Lindgren would complement each other as presenters at the first Symposium.

I recall being greeted by some mild misgivings (Do we *need* a Symposium? What about the cost? And so on.) when I proposed our idea to the Executive Board at that November's convention, but we won the Board of Governors' approval, and everything fell into place for that inaugural Symposium that was held at the Grand Cypress resort near Orlando the following February.

I stepped down from the Council chairmanship in the fall of '92 but eagerly assumed the job of editing each year's Symposium video production, which eventually came to nearly 30 hours of finished tape over the decade.

This project was very different from making the *Introduction to Dressage* video from scratch (which I described in an earlier story). In these productions the commercial film crew recorded every moment of each Symposium, often with three cameras. We did live switching to lay down the best video track but kept all the source tapes to intercut better views after the fact. So each Symposium was documented with about 16 running hours of tape (times three).

My main job was to make three stand-alone one hour stories out of all this material. In most cases it was like culling all but the premier steers from a herd, leaving the most meaningful themes and most useful exercises to chronicle the best of the sessions. One or two years it was more like trying to find enough pickles to make a picnic, but hey, so it goes.

107

Aside from sorting through the haystack to find the "good stuff," I also had to determine edit points that, when strung back to back to back, would make a fairly seamless audio track that needed a minimum of distracting voice-over. Each tape required finding dozens of these, and to get it sounding just right, I would sit in my living room and play short segments back and forth, over and over, listening for the best places to "cut and paste."

Back in the spring of 1996, we had a live-in teenaged working student of considerable talent who kept her horses with us. She and Susan would often sit in the next room trying to work or study and unavoidably had to endure the repetitive audio from my project. At the time Courtney was doing Advanced Young Riders and trying to qualify for the NAYRC. We were up in Georgia celebrating a particularly successful show day, having dinner with her, her mom, and a few other riders of ours. As we left the restaurant, Courtney grabbed one of the hostess-proffered helium-filled balloons, inhaled its contents in the parking lot, and in a gratingly nasal, gas-induced Daffy Duck voice performed a perfect word-for-word recitation of a Robert Dover monologue from the Symposium tape she'd heard me working on for so many hours.

And you wonder why I don't have children?

53
"Queen Elizabeth II Has Spent Hours with the Prototype," Says Hi Tech Video Gaming Retailer. "It's Boffo!" Queen Declares.

The Nintendo Corporation this week announced plans to introduce a new 2009 edition of Wii-compatible software called Wii Stable Girl. In a promotional brochure distributed by the company's marketing arm, Nintendo spokesperson Lenore Drickle proclaimed, "We are aiming for a new demographic. Without having to leave the comfort of your patio or exercise room, it will be possible for suburban housewives and urban apartment-dwellers to mimic every aspect of taking care of a six-stall barn of spoiled and obstreperous dressage horses."

Drickle points to an updated, more powerful graphics package that "puts you right behind the horse." The game may be played by one to four participants. ScoreCheck™ permits points to be awarded for how early you arise to feed the virtual horses, dump and refill virtual water buckets, and muck the virtual stalls. The Wii Remote is the primary controller for the fifth generation console that best displays the new game's features. The remote uses combinations of built-in accelerometers and infrared detection to sense its position in 3D space when pointed at the LEDs within the Sensor Bar. The controlling device is specially programmed to require the same kinesthetic wrist twist with your virtual pitchfork that produces accuracy in the real world.

The controller connects to the console using Bluetooth and incorporates rumble as well as an internal speaker to replicate the sound of impatiently pawing hooves.

Nintendo also revealed a commercial tie-in with a joint-venture startup of former Nike employees and the Portland Cement Company. This group will manufacture concrete shoes to be worn by gamers to enhance the similarities to actual stable work.

The company is also exploring a proposal by Bio-nano-tech giant MetricPest to include downloadable coupons on its website, redeemable for micro-robotic fly-facsimiles that could be released in the virtual barn space.

The console, incidentally, features parental controls that can be engaged by a husband or any other individual displaying enough sense to keep his wife or child from straying down the tawdry path to equine management and financial and physical ruin, whether virtual or otherwise.

Nintendo is exploring the viability of spinoff companion products—Wii Hay Delivery Man and Wii Farrier—in test markets around the country.

54
Disaster Planning

A well known clinician travels the U.S. giving seminars on positive thinking in dressage. Another Olympic veteran counsels, "Don't think of what might go wrong, people; think of what should go right."

This may be all well and good, but I look at it a different way. Confidence shouldn't come from wishful thinking; it should derive from competence that, in turn, comes from knowing how to deal with any circumstance that might arise.

OK, I agree that you shouldn't go down the centerline defensively, just waiting for the axe to fall. But as any judge will tell you, for each movement and each figure they see, they can easily list a couple of specific faults that they'll view over and over from one rider to the next. If you know what things typically can go wrong and you practice what to do about them or how to avoid them, you refine your coping skills to nip the problem in the bud. Knowing how to skip those "Uh oh, what do I do now?" moments goes a long way towards building the reality-based confidence a good rider should possess.

You're probably familiar with that line that "piloting an airplane is hours of boredom interspersed with moments of sheer terror." As a consequence, pilots are drilled on emergency procedures until they can react to disaster reflexively, instantly, and practically in their sleep. The kinds of dressage "disasters" we're looking at are minor in comparison. The neck overbends in a shoulder-in. The rider collapses her inside hip and takes the outside leg off. But the point is, if you know these things go wrong all the time, then you have a before-the-fact strategy to fix the problem and you aren't left wondering, "Hmmm, what's the matter here?"

As a rider, you should be able to make a short list of common faults for every movement. Try that and then go to the German manual **Principles of Riding** and see if you were right!

55

Navel Gazing
Don't Give Up the Ship... or Your Outside Leg

If I had to pick any one personality trait, one quality, that would best serve you as a dressage aspirant, I'd most likely choose *self awareness*. It's been said that the learning of many skills can be divided into four stages.

They are Unconscious Incompetence, Conscious Incompetence, Conscious Competence, and finally Unconscious Competence. That last stage is where everything flows so naturally and automatically that you don't have to think of it at all. Please let me be the first to know when you've achieved that.

The first stage is one of blissful ignorance. Since you don't know what you're missing, what you are doing seems pretty good to you. Most riders who are trying to climb the ladder dwell in the middle two stages. Either things aren't working but by now you know it, or perhaps they're starting to work, yet it takes a heck of a conscious effort to make them happen correctly.

Some facets of self awareness are beyond our ability to affect. In those cases you've either got it or you don't. To compensate for my personal shortcomings in this department, I have taught myself to say *Man kharam* which means "I am an idiot" in Persian. Other more specific self awarenesses can be learned— "the spectacles, testicles, wallet, and watch" gesture that men learn to conduct before walking out the door for work in the morning, for example. Here there are numerous dressage applications that can improve your riding skills.

You just have to remember to ask yourself the relevant questions every so often. In fact, very often!

"When was the last time that I did something with my inside rein?" isn't a very good question since everyone *always* uses their inside rein. A better question in this case might be, "When was the last time I DIDN'T do something with it?" An equally good question on a 20-meter circle, during a shoulder-in, or in a turn on the forehand is "When was the last time my outside leg said anything to my horse?"

It's a pretty good bet that all your body parts and all your aids have a role to play in whatever exercise you're doing. Check in on them and make sure they're present and on the job.

How can you remember to make these checks? It's been suggested that you adopt a "trigger" to remind you—every time you are headed east, every time you see a bird or a car goes past. Find a crutch to jog you into checking and soon it will become automatic.

56
Party Time!

When you try to ride correctly, all those instructions run through your head about body alignment, balance, lifted ribs that make a shock absorber between your upper body and your hips, and on and on. Lots of times I see people so busy "equitating," that they can barely focus on riding their horse.

Here's a simple piece of advice. Your upper body position as you canter or sit to the trot is one you've used lots of other times in a different context. Imagine you're about to entertain guests at a moderately formal dinner party. Your boss (and her husband) are coming over for cocktails and a meal. It's just dressy enough to require real napkins, let's say. When you go to the front door to greet their arrival, you assume a respectful, upright posture. You neither look like a rigid mannequin holding your breath with the coat hanger still stuck inside your shirt, nor do you slouch to the door, hunched forward with one hip cocked and a wad of gum in your mouth. If you can think of an in-between posture that's both erect and natural, you've got it.

Then, as long as we're in the party mode, imagine it's a bigger gathering that you're hosting. Since it's your party, you can't hide off in the corner and be passive. As the Perfect Host(ess), you have to mingle, introduce guests to one

Steve Waller

another, play the scintillating conversationalist to spark their interest in one another, and move along to another cluster of people. This same characteristic will serve you well if you apply it to how you entertain and motivate your horse. Clearly you don't want to overwhelm or intimidate him, but likewise you don't want to drone on in a monotone that puts him to sleep. Mastering the art of conversation with your horse will make him want to invite you to *his* party in return.

57
Sounds That Emanate, Escalate, Degenerate; Civil Disobedience Ensues

In principle, a voice that projects well is an asset when you teach for a living. Some of us just have trouble turning that voice off, which has a way of annoying and embarrassing one's companions (to say nothing of one's spouse) if you're in a restaurant any more sophisticated than Chuckie Cheese.

At my first real teaching job back in the '70s, I spent many hours in an outdoor arena bounded on the north by a thick copse of trees that separated us from the next farm. When I was preparing to leave there for a new position

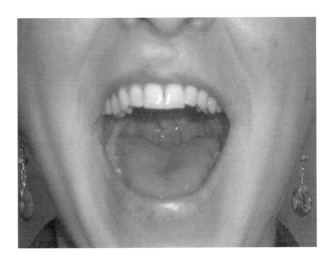

after six years, my students held a going away party and included the northern neighbors on the invite list.

At the party the neighbor approached me. "Thank you very much for all the things I've learned about riding," she said. "I've stood at my kitchen sink for the last six years and I've heard every word you said." (Oops!)

Another time, I was conducting an Instructor Workshop in Minnesota. The father of one of the young instructors had been recruited to manage the AV cart. As I began to speak, I saw him frantically trying to adjust various dials on the amplifier console.

"What's wrong," I asked him.

"I'm trying to figure out how to turn down the gain on the wireless mike," he replied.

"Oh," I managed. "I haven't turned the microphone on yet." (Oops Number Two!)

More recently, I encountered another complainer about my vocalizations. One particular Florida show manager had a "thing" about what he perceived as decorum. He felt that the warm-up arena should radiate the same sacred ambiance as the 18th green at St. Andrews. Maybe a few whispers would be allowed, but more appropriate would be the universal use of handheld walkie talkies by the coaches, and belt-mounted receivers by the riders.

My own feeling is that these devices are more a hindrance than a boon. Each rider becomes locked in her own world and follows the voice in her ear like a Stepford-esque automaton with no regard for what anyone around her is doing. Likewise, the coaches are single-mindedly driving their own little charges around with no sense of what their peers are telling the other riders to do and with no hope of sharing the space in a logical way and avoiding collisions.

When informed that acquiring such a device would be desirable, the next day I brought a Spam can to the ring, taped it up with a coat hanger antenna, held it to my mouth, and continued to shout my instructions as usual.

I remain unconvinced that the "modern" way is better.

I do think that Theater of the Absurd is the best way to deal with unreasonable demands. Even if it doesn't ameliorate the situation, it makes you feel a lot better. Once we arrived at a showgrounds in New England to find that the Technical Delegate had taken it upon herself to institute a protective helmet rule. I certainly can't argue with the desirability of wearing a hardhat while riding. But in Live Free or Die New Hampshire, it seemed to me that if the management wanted to enforce such a rule, they should have put it in their prize list. Since I was showing my horse in the FEI and planning to wear a top hat on show day, I hadn't even thought to pack a helmet. The management had no opinion one way or the other. This was all about TD Power.

My solution was to borrow our dog's tin water bowl and duct tape it to my head with several wrappings over the top of the inverted bowl and around under my chin. It lent a special sort of WW I doughboy look to us, I thought.

The TD, though she didn't think this was especially humorous, was astute enough to know she was being mocked, felt the tide of rider opinion turning against her, and rescinded her edict.

I should be ashamed for resisting falling into sheep-like behavior in situations like these, but hey, we grew up in the '60s. Read on. We will rejoice more below as humble mortals again confront The Machine.

58

The Devil Made Me Do It

I don't really think it's the rules that drive me crazy. It's the people who enforce them and who act like arbitrary looniness is a sacrament of officialdom. This observation inevitably brings me to the rules (and related urban legends) surrounding the wearing of bridle numbers.

Really, I'm fine if the USEF wants to be able to identify each horse at every moment. I can see reasons why. For a time, though, people were being threatened with elimination if their horses weren't wearing their numbers in the wash rack. That seemed extreme to me till I observed the TD at the motel pool with his wallet in his swimming trunks.

One particularly Germanic Technical Delegate was forever wanting to punish owners whose horses were wearing just one bridle number. He and I went round and round about the wording in the rules—"horses must wear numbers"—and whether that implied that each must wear two or just that *they* (collectively) had to wear *their* numbers (individually). At the time many

115

shows were only issuing one per entry so enforcement of his interpretation was pretty problematic anyway.

I'm afraid a part of me has always been like the goggle-eyed kid in the Far Side cartoons using his magnifying glass to "warm up" the ants on the sidewalk. Klaus, the TD, was such an easy target (and if I may say so, a very deserving one). I knew he was in the show office and I couldn't help but parade my horse in front of the window with both my bridle numbers on the opposite side from his vantage point. Of course he came rushing out to scold me, and I was able to say, "But he IS wearing both his numbers. Your rule doesn't say anything about *where*."

The next day I bent the metal tabs on my numbers over backwards and used a magic marker to convert the "216"s to "CCXVI"s. Klaus's reaction in his thick accent, "Mister Vood, you are not keeping with zee zspirit of zee rrrulez. You are zee reazon zat zee rrrule book iz zo thick!"

The final word on this matter was heard the following spring when I judged a show 800 miles away at Lake Erie College in Ohio. Waiting for classes to get underway Sunday morning, I was standing with the Director of the Riding Program at the college, the Show Manager, and the show's TD. Someone was remarking how beautiful it had been in the stillness of dawn with a herd of wild deer grazing just behind the indoor arena.

"Yes," another voice added, "but if Klaus were the TD, he'd have made them all put on bridle numbers!"

59

Hear [Her] Roar

When I teach my regular lessons, I'm blessed with some fairly sophisticated riders and talented horses. At clinics the fare is more varied. One 13-year-old girl came into a clinic lesson with a "project" Arabian. The horse was middle-aged and had had some years of practice getting his own way. He was very lazy to the leg and would only bend one direction, and that was only because he was so hollow to that side that he couldn't have been straight.

116

His rider was very sweet but passive beyond measure, and it looked like it was going to be a very long 45 minutes for me. Her making the horse round was out of the question. A lively trot wasn't going to happen. Steering was unlikely other than in its very broadest definition. The kid just seemed helpless.

We pursued attention and energy through a bunch of different exercises, more or less to no avail. Finally I called her over to me.

"Shawna," I asked, "Is your bedroom painted pink?"

She looked a little dumbfounded and answered hesitantly, "Yes."

"And do you have a canopied four poster bed with chiffon ruffles around the top?"

"Yes," meekly.

"And do you have your walls covered with shelves filled with stuffed animals?"

"Um, yes."

Raising my voice, I shouted (kindly), "Well, for heaven's sake, could you please just GET A LIFE??!"

She seemed startled but took my remonstrations in stride. Later, as the lesson was wrapping up pleasantly, I gave her some homework till the next time.

At that first lesson she'd been accompanied by her dad. The next month she arrived with her mother instead, and the first thing Shawna did was show me her fingernails. She'd done them for me in Goth Black nail polish.

And she rode like a Changed Person! She could make her horse go forward. She could leg yield down the track nose to the wall, make a partial turn on the forehand and leg yield back. Her horse really behaved!

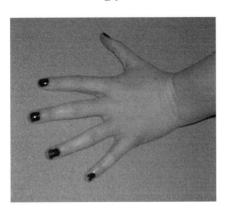

As her Mom said to me afterwards, "I haven't seen Shawna ride for a long time, but *she can make Princess go where she wants now!*"

It's a Concept, I thought. It could have happened years ago, but better now than never!

60

Good News, Bad News

There's a joke about a shipful of galley slaves. Each slave ship had a crew member called a Beater whose job it was to beat a drum at the cadence in which all the slaves were supposed to row. Otherwise their oars could become entangled and throw the whole operation out of kilter.

So one day at lunchtime the Beater stands up in front of the slaves and says, "Men, I have some good news and some bad news.

"The good news is that the Captain has decreed that you'll each have an extra ration of wine for lunch.

"The bad news is that after lunch, the Captain wants to water ski again!"

There are good news and bad news moments in dressage also. When you ride a circle, the good news is that the sameness of the bend and a consistent, unchanging line can steady a horse and make him settle into a better rhythm.

With some horses, however, these same results of circle riding are the *bad* news as well. If your horse is strong or bullying, if he likes to lean on your hand, tune you out, or fall on his outside shoulder, circles can be just too much of an invitation for evasion for him to turn down.

A very good solution is to make your horse go on an octagon instead. In a "stop sign" shape, make a figure whose overall dimension is 20 meters across. Begin by making four or five straight strides on the track centered on B, then a 45 degree turn and another four or five strides straight. One more

45 degree turn and you'll be making the next straight side perpendicular to the centerline and straddled across it at the same point a 20-meter circle would. Keep doing this. After eight sides and eight turns you'll be back where you started.

The benefit of this exercise is that the doldrums that a circle can sometimes

create are avoided. Instead of your horse being held in a static balance between centrifugal force and your pulling inner rein, the octagonal figure affords you eight lovely opportunities to make a half halt that will put him back under himself and in line.

When you've learned how to get into his mind this much, you can start to make a polygon with even more corners. Ultimately, your figure will have as many sides and corners as the number of strides it takes to complete the full 360 degrees around, and to everyone watching, you will have ridden a well-planned, well-balanced circle.

61

Can't Help It—A Serious Moment!
(Maybe Something in the Drinking Water)

Like the typical dressage person, I am currently busy taking myself too seriously; so, while in that mode, here are a couple of general observations about our sport and us. I think we all go through phases of introspective PETA-esque questioning: *Should we ride them at all? Should we even own them? Should they live in barns and not roam free in herds?*

Most of us get over that part. But we shouldn't get so jaded or callous as to overlook the civilization-altering mystery of why horses ever put up with us at all. Given what so many horses have granted us so willingly, it is imperative not to lose sight of what we owe them in return. Feed and shelter and care are obvious. I'm thinking more about respecting them as creatures. From a poster hanging in our tack room quoting Henry Beston in **The Outermost House**:

Remote from universal nature, and living by complicated artifice, man in civilization surveys the [horse] through the glass of his knowledge and sees thereby a feather magnified and the whole image in distortion. We patronize them for their incompleteness, for their having taken form so far below ourselves. And therein we err, and greatly err. For the animal shall not be measured by man. In a world older and more complete than ours they move finished and complete, gifted with the extensions of the senses we have lost or never attained, living by voices we shall never hear. They are not brethren, they are not underlings; they are other nations, caught with ourselves in the net of life and time, fellow prisoners of the splendor and travail of the earth.

In practical terms it's about keeping our relationship with horses in perspective so that they never become mere vehicles for our personal vainglories. In this way we won't let the game we play with horses distort our sense of fairness to them or of what's right.

At one point years ago my Dad (a mechanical engineer by profession) lost his job as the result of a corporate merger where his New Boss gobbled up the R&D Department that he headed. I said to him at the time, "Well at least *I* can never lose *my* job from technological obsolescence." His rejoinder was, "Yeah, that's because it's already been obsolete for 200 years!"

I try to remember those words when I get red-faced ranting about one injustice or another in the dressage world or if I start to pressure my students about things they can't control or especially when riders or parents or spouses get massively full of themselves or overly imbued with the "life and death" consequences of their competitive exploits or travails.

It is only a GAME, People! When dressage gets you too whacked-out, go save some whales or hammer a house together for needy people or just take a breath and admire the sunset or the sound of your horse chewing contentedly on his hay in a quiet barn late in the evening. This last always restores my balance when my dressage gyroscope has gone awry.

62

Always a Libertine,
Now a Libertarian, Too

You've probably seen the proposed rule change that would require riders to qualify with scores at a given level before being permitted to move up to the next level. The actual specifics are a bit more complicated than that, but you get the idea.

Frankly, without wanting to sound too much like a heartless proponent of the Free Market *Über alles*, this goes just a little too far towards the Dressage Welfare State for my taste.

I appreciate a desire to protect the horses from bad riding. I understand that in the best possible world, riders would work their way up through the levels and never try to go beyond their sphere of competence, mastering each concept appropriately before challenging themselves with the next one. But I don't think the proposal will accomplish any of that.

Bad riders will still ride badly at whatever level they're in. Not-so-good riders on fancy, trained horses will get the scores required to move up even if they still have bad hands and are semi-clueless about the real meaning of the sport they're trying to figure out. I'd be inclined to add that good riders on not-too-talented horses will be penalized, except the proposed scores you'll need are low enough to make the whole thing moot.

I suspect that one part of the group lobbying for this change is the judges who are tired of looking at less than stellar performances. My suggestion to them is "Suck it up and judge!" While I wish everyone I judged would ride well, I personally don't mind judging the struggles of people finding their way through the dressage maze towards enlightenment. Meanwhile, if a rider's new schoolmaster can do the PSG and the rider has only ever shown First Level, I don't see why they should have to wrestle with Second Level in a snaffle just to get to where the horse has been competing in his double bridle for the past ten years. And speaking of the snaffle versus double bridle controversy, I don't think you're doing some stiff jawed old trouper a favor by making his rider be hauled around in a snaffle at Third (or Fourth) Level.

Ultimately it's about the judging. If the ride is good, you're supposed to get rewarded. If you can't make things work—no matter what level, no matter what pre-qualification, no matter what bit—you should hear about it from the judge. And if you're smart enough to be listening, you should re-evaluate what you've entered and whether you're sufficiently prepared to do the kind of test that won't pain the audience, whether it's the judge, your coach, or just the family dog.

63

Schooling Show Mischief

I was judging a schooling show in east Texas when a woman I knew came down the centerline to do First Level Test 4. The show manager had just informed me that permission had been granted for this woman's test to be called in Spanish. A Mexican gentleman, whose children had come "up north" for the show, then stationed himself at B and in a striking baritone, boomed out each successive command.

I was quite tickled by all this because while the woman rode through the pattern flawlessly, I knew her well enough to be certain that her linguistic skills in the Spanish tongue were less than zero, and that the reader's utterances to her amounted to total gibberish.

An "A+" for theatrics! You have to like that in a rider.

Another time in Minnesota I was judging a schooling show, and a novice rider was doing an old Training Test 2. Part way through the test she took the canter and didn't notice it was the wrong lead. When I judge, if you take the wrong lead and correct it, it's worth a 4. If you don't correct it, the score drops one number. The next movement was a 20-meter circle and the horse was still happily sailing along on the outside lead. By then, that's another point lower—a 2. Not being able to *get* the correct lead is one thing; not knowing you should be trying after this long is a larger fault.

But then the horse began diving into the hand, which set off a binge of swearing from the rider. Voice! Two more points off and we're at 0. Not to leave any stone unturned, she then forgot the second half of her circle altogether. I had to blow the whistle for an Error and she was at two below 0! Even measuring in Fahrenheit, that was a new record for me.

Later in the ride her horse had reverted to his normal, more sedentary demeanor and he moseyed across the diagonal in a very sleepy and casual free walk. I said to the scribe, "5, Somnambulant."

She answered back, "I don't know how to spell that."

Upon reflection, neither did I. So when the rider made her final salute at G, we stopped her and offered her two make-up bonus points if she could spell the word for us.

Turns out she *could,* which resulted in an additional line on the bottom of the score sheet. Right under the line for Error Deductions came a new line: Spelling Rewards.

Then there was Louisiana—a pleasant little schooling show that was chock full of Intro Tests, Green-as-Grass, and Novice Training One and Two. Finally around four in the afternoon we were about to judge a Second Level test. My scribe was very good. We'd worked together often in the past, and I said to her, "Do you think you can do this next one in Roman Numerals?"

"No problem," she giggled.

So the test was judged as usual with all the normal comments except each score block said IV or VII or whatever, instead of 4 or 7. When I wrote out the Collectives at the bottom, I did the coefficients myself to be sure we sent them in correctly: XIV, XII, X, XII. I appended my name, watched the little runner kid deliver it to the scorer, and waited.

No reaction.

Finally, I strolled over to her during the break and asked, "Say, did you get that Second Level test sheet?"

"Oh, yes," she said breathlessly. "I'm just so and so's mother and I've never done this job before. I didn't realize the upper levels have to be scored that way!"

64
Don't Tease Me, Bro'

I was judging in Nashville at a state of the art facility with an air conditioned coliseum and several other covered arenas. My post was at an arena on "the back forty," and at 7:30 a.m., I was just about to toot my duck call to summon the first rider of the day when the PA sprang to life, announcing that the EMT had not arrived yet, and according to USEF rules, the show was On Hold until he showed up.

Some minutes passed and the announcer reiterated the problem and assured the riders that we would get started and be back on schedule shortly but not until the missing medical tech appeared.

Another 10 minutes dragged by—situation unchanged. My scribe was the former club president and someone who had organized clinics for me in the past. I asked if she knew the show manager's cell number and asked her to dial it for me.

Taking the phone, I raised my voice an octave and said into it, "Hello? Mrs. Donovan? This is the EMT."

"Where in the world are you?" she began in a not terribly charitable tone.

"Oh, I'm coming. Don't worry," I answered.

"Worry?" she replied as I felt her rising blood pressure practically vibrate the receiver in my hand. "I have 200 people waiting who can't do anything till you get here!"

"Well," I said, "It's Saturday morning and I always go to Wal-Mart on Saturdays. Is it OK if I show up around 10:30?"

At this point she started to sputter incoherently and I could imagine a cloud of smoke coming off the top of her head. "Sandy, this is really Bill Woods," I admitted.

All the while, the office where she'd been holding her half of our conversation was crammed with competitors who had been overhearing the exchange. As you'd guess, the story of the ruse spread quickly and got some laughs. The manager threatened first not to feed me and then never to speak to me again, but all was forgotten when the EMT drove in a few minutes later. Seems that when the starting time was pushed up a half hour earlier, no one had remembered to inform him of the change. He thought he had to be there by eight, and being a conscientious kind of guy, by golly, he was!

65
Glory Days

Back "in the day" when we lived in Massachusetts, Susan and I put out the NEDA newsletter faithfully though somewhat irregularly. We stole as many funny ideas as we could and tried to make our little "cut, paste, and press-type offering" something that our 1500 readers might look forward to. There was Susan's actual correspondence with Andy Rooney, assorted goofy contests, theme issues like the Boss one where every headline was a title of a

Springsteen song, and the Rocky Horror issue, where a running blood-red masthead proclaimed "A Tip of the Hat—at the Late Night, Double Feature, Picture Show."

The newsletter, you see, was "A Tip of the Hat." Its parent publication, a glossy yearbook type magazine, being bigger, was a full *Salute*. From time to time our mischief leaked into the big mag too. We had been to New Orleans to represent NEDA at the USDF Convention and had slipped into the traveling animatronic dinosaur exhibit next to the old Jax brewery while we were there.

Coincidentally, Susan had just purchased a 17.3 hand show horse whom she'd nicknamed "Dino." This was the photo that I sent in to *The Salute*, captioned: *Susan Woods with her new Swedish Warmblood, Dino.*

Another time, the editor of *The Salute* wanted to do a feature article on Those Woodses. She called and said, "Hey, I could ask you a bunch of questions, but you can probably think of better ones to ask yourselves. Why don't you just do that?"

So we more or less pretended to be interviewed, which of course involved a lot of complicated running back and forth from one side of the dining room table to the other depending on whether we were asking ourselves or answering.

One of the questions was "How did you two meet?" The answer, a total fabrication, we purloined from lyrics from a Springsteen song called "Racing in the Street":

BILL: I met her on the strip three years ago in a Camaro with this dude from L.A.
SUSAN: He blew that Camaro off his back and stole my little heart away.

Along with the rest of the article, this little exchange came out in print and went out to the membership. About that time, I had started to go to a new barn to do lessons, and one of my regular students who'd recently moved her horse there said there was a teenage girl who wanted to know if I'd autograph her copy.

We were introduced and as I was penning some sort of "Good luck with your pretty mare" kind of message, she said to me, "I really loved your story. And the way you met each other was *so romantic!*"

Indeed.

66

The (Dressage) Princess and the Pea

I admit to being somewhat bemused by riders who repeatedly screech to a stop in the middle of a lesson in order to raise or shorten their stirrup a half hole.

It seems to me that if you have a camcorder on a tripod, you make the camera level and you adjust the legs differently as required to keep it that way. Similarly, if my cousin Tiger hits into the rough and has an uneven lie, he keeps his shoulders and hips level and adjusts his legs to keep his swing on plane.

When you ride, your base of support is the bottom side of your pelvis (those seatbones) and your upper (don't you dare grip!) thighs. You distribute your weight symmetrically over them and let your legs fall into place below.

At a clinic once, I needed to get on a student's horse. He was a little guy, a Fourth Level Arabian-Quarter Horse cross. She was a fairly short rider. As I was lowering my stirrup on the near side, I called across to her, "Five holes."

When I got on, I discovered that she'd accidentally raised the off side leather that amount instead of lowering it. She started to be embarrassed, but I told her, "Just leave them that way. It doesn't matter."

Then I proceeded to ride him, the left stirrup ten holes longer that the right one, and did his canter half passes, flying changes, and counter changes.

I saw a more dramatic demonstration at a Trainer's Conference in West Palm a few years ago. Klaus Balkenhol was on a Grand Prix horse, passaging. Then without the horse losing the rhythm, Balkenhol leaned far to the left, leaned far to the right, even took one leg out in space. And the horse just kept on working.

This isn't to downplay the importance of refinement or subtlety. Sitting centered with legs and stirrups that match is the right picture to aim for. But don't get so distracted by what you ought to regard as little things that you can't focus on what does matter.

And realize that if your horse knows you know how to ride, he's smart enough to discriminate between when you make an incidental movement (like leaning down to get your water bottle) versus weighting your seatbone to displace him laterally. While you want him intently on the aids, you want him to give you a break if you have to sneeze or turn to find your cell phone in your back pocket. This laptop I'm using seems to respond to the keys I strike even if I don't mean to hit them. Fortunately for me, my horse is a little smarter than that.

67

Readin', 'Riting and 'Rithmetic

These three stories really don't have a darn thing in common. They just fit the title.

Readin'

In North Carolina I judged an exceptionally well-ridden First Level Test 4. The rider was a professional. A besmocked woman who was clearly the horse's proud owner and groom read the test for her. Unfortunately, she read First Level Test 3.

Fairly early on, she had looked up, discovered the rider wasn't doing what she had just read, and hurried down her sheet to where the rider seemed to be. She would pick up from there, only to see the rider again deviate from what she had next said. Three more times the reader thought she had "caught up" and three more times she became increasingly frustrated as her rider just kept doing "the wrong thing." When, at last, the test was over, I congratulated the reader on what a fine job she'd done but did mention that it would have been even better if she and her rider would agree on which test they were doing.

'Riting

At a Louisiana horse trials my scribe and I were observed to be misbehaving. Surely that was untrue. (And don't call me Shirley). There is a certain protocol for how you mark "errors" on a test sheet. It's important that they are brought to the scorer's attention in a way that the deduction is made and made only once. Back "in the day" judges sometimes wrote "-2" in the block where the error occurred but that led to confusion as to whether or not the deduction had already been made when the score for the movement was written down. The convention that was informally adopted was that over on the left hand side of the sheet, the scribe would write the word "ERROR" in very large letters. Then after the test was finished, the judge would total up whatever error points had accrued (2 for the first, 4 more for the second, elimination for the third) and put that number in the designated block at the bottom of the sheet so the scorer could make the subtraction from the overall total she arrived at. Never able to leave well enough alone, the Bureaucracy decreed that when the scribe wrote the word "ERROR," it should be done with a red pen.
Because.

I was aware of all this but wasn't feeling all that submissive myself; so when a rider went off course, my scribe wrote "ERROR" on the sheet and I put the correct deduction unmistakably in the box, *but we didn't use our red pen.* This was back when the horse trials still let us have a walkie talkie (When they discovered we were using it to sing to the other stations on the net, it was confiscated) so very shortly we were reprimanded over the airwaves for our chromatic indiscretion.

The next time there was an error, my scribe still used her blue pen, but I added parenthetically in blue "This is red." That drew another call demanding actual red ink.

To make up for our oversight, I had my scribe write the next test entirely in red. This earned us yet a third conference on the radio. In the spirit of compromise I asked my scribe if she could write out the next test in alternate colors, which isn't that easy to do in "real" time. Try it.

128

So, for instance, I said, "6, Needs more energy."

My scribe would write "6" in blue, and then leaving spaces would write "N E S O E N R Y" in the comment block. She would quickly go back with her red pen and fill in "E D M R E E G" in between. She did this for every block. We sent that test in and it must have really impressed the scorers because the TD came all the way out to our ring to scold us in person. She really shouldn't have bothered. The dressage phase of this event was being held on October 31st—Halloween—and for the occasion I was wearing a leather headband sort of contraption that held my ceramic devil's horns in place. When the TD knocked on our window and looked in, my horns and I smiled back at her. She stared a moment, then decided just to wish us a good day and went on her way.

'Rithmetic

It took me a little while to come up with a good "'Rithmetic" story to complete the trilogy, but here you go.

Riders who get past Fourth Level Test 1 have to do tempi changes, and that means they have to COUNT. It sounds so easy when you're just watching at ringside, but many riders find it way stressful when they're also trying to keep their horse straight, balanced, attentive, expressive, and all the other things that critical judges, coaches, and random hangers-on complain about.

Don't underestimate the difficulty. I taught a woman who captained L-1011s for Delta on the Great Circle route to the Soviet Union. She also played classical violin. She told me that learning to ride FEI level tests was the hardest thing she'd ever done in her life! Another student of mine was a microbiologist, had her PhD, and was chairman of her department at the university. She needed a year to figure out how to count her tempis. One other girl got them right almost immediately. Then she started thinking about them, and the knack deserted her for months.

I did have one Young Rider who showed special promise. Almost like an artistic savant, she could do the fours, threes, and twos correctly the very first time and almost every time. For her it was just no big deal.

Once a rider gets confident with lines of tempis, it's time to play. I have one skillful student with an older horse that gets too wise for his own good. I was able to trick him and keep him listening honestly by having her ride 4-3-2-1 and then back up 1-2-3-4. That's much harder for the rider than just to do a line of five changes every fourth stride. From there we started doing zip codes and phone numbers. (My Zip is 3-4-4-8-2.)

By the way, if you decide to try it yourself, a phone number complete with area code requires a pretty long driveway!

68

Where the Women Are Strong, the Men Are Good Looking, And All the Mots Are Bon

I used to do some clinics near Huntsville, AL, which is home to the Marshall Space Flight Center, made famous by Dr. Werner Von Braun and his colleagues. There they developed the booster engines that sent our first satellite into space, as well as the Saturn V that put Americans on the moon. The woman I sometimes stayed with was an engineer in "real life" who worked for Rocketdyne on main engine upgrades for NASA's space shuttle. Her bookcases at home were filled with technical tomes that, when I opened one, contained only page-long formulae and very few recognizable words.

The horse she rode was a Trakehner mare who could get her goat at times. More often than not, the problem was that her rider just got trying too hard, thinking too much, and just plain getting too much in her own way to be effective. Observing all this, I called her over to me one day, looked up sincerely and was able to say with a straight face, "Heather, you know, riding isn't Rocket Science!"

At one clinic out West an auditor approached me to say that she had recently purchased a horse that I was familiar with.

"The former owner showed me a video of you working with him," she told me.

"Ah ha," seemed like the only appropriate rejoinder.

"But you said one thing about him that I didn't understand," she continued hopefully. "You called him 'the Maynard G. Krebs of Dressage.'"

130

You have to be of a certain age to remember who this was. I was not about to tell her that Maynard was a Bob Denver (who later played Gilligan) character on the ancient TV show called *The Many Loves of Dobie Gillis*. Maynard was a sweatshirted, goateed beatnik who, anytime anyone even mentioned the topic in passing, shrieked "Work!" in a horrified tone. Unfortunately, this reaction pretty much summed up the personality of the horse she had just bought.

At a clinic in north Texas, a woman brought her Arabian into the arena. He was a pleasant enough horse but he carried himself like a bad caricature of a Quarter Horse who'd swallowed the calavetti pole. His topline was one continuous horizontal bar from his tail to the tip of his nose.

After watching him go for a few minutes, I called his rider in to me and began, "What we'll do first is start to soften him and shape his frame a little more. Let's put him on a circle with his front end on an inner track. Then we can yield him into the outside rein and ask him to flex more at the poll."

"I don't understand what's wrong," she responded.

Cutting to the chase, I said, "I mean he's sticking his nose out"

"He is not," she replied, "He has a dished face!"

69
Things That Go Bump in the Day

Earlier, I spoke of dressage as a non-verbal language and talked about the aids as verbs, adjectives, and adverbs. When you're on your horse in the arena "writing," don't forget the punctuation. Intersperse commas and periods (and maybe an occasional exclamation point) in your discourse to regain your horse's attention and to adjust his balance. Remember to avoid those treacherous run-on sentences.

Alternatively, if writing isn't your "thing," maybe what you learned in your youth as a teenaged mall rat can finally be of use. Not the part at the Piercing Pagoda. Not the part at the food court. I'm talking *parking lot*.

If you have a horse that gets cruising with you, think of driving down the fire lane outside the mall entrance. That's where mall architects always put

those raised speed bumps so when you hit the white haired lady pedestrians, you hit them more slowly.

Unless you're a guy, a speed bump momentarily slows you down. You pump the brakes and make a slight hesitation so your head doesn't bounce off the roof of your car. As you go over each bump, you feel the car rock back.

The reason I make this analogy is that I find riders all the time who think that they're making half halts. They do some sort of "squeeze–give" thing with their hand and figure they're fulfilling their responsibility. On the other hand, if I put them on a 20-meter circle and tell them they should make their horse react for the speed bump that they hit each time they cross over the centerline, then they think less of their own action and concentrate instead on weighing the physical reaction from their horse.

A few extra thoughts must accompany this image because, of course, a half halt isn't just slowing down. There has to be a "re-inflating" component that keeps the horse energized, uphill, and in front of the leg. Nonetheless, if you can't negotiate your speed bumps properly, you don't have your horse as much on the aids as he should be.

70
The Tale of the Tape
Episode Four

Every four years, not long after the USEF puts out a new set of dressage tests, a DVD follows that shows how the movements are supposed to be performed and what the tests look like.

This idea originated with the 1995 [then] AHSA tests. The camera crew that videoed the 1995 National Symposium was already assembled at the LA Equestrian Center in Griffith Park, so the idea was to do the shoot at the same venue the day after the symposium ended. Their plan was to assemble some good horses and riders, do the tests, and hand the results to a committee of four senior judges who would record a voice track with suitable commentary.

As you may have noticed in your own life, committees aren't exactly the most efficient way to get a lot of tasks accomplished. This was no exception. After the nature of the rat's nest they'd created became apparent, the USDF called me. I had been involved all along with editing the Symposium tapes. The request was could I "do something" with the video they'd made for this project? Time was of the essence, they added, because the Office had already publicized and taken order money for *On the Levels*, even though it didn't exist yet.

This was a project that appealed to me very much. Before the phone call I had already begun an informal backyard version of the same thing that I was making for my own students and to show at clinic evenings. I even had the entire script outlined.

But problems arose immediately when the window dubs from Burbank arrived in the Express mail. Some rides were duplicates. Some rides were awful. When I pieced everything together, I had just about enough usable footage to cover Training through Fourth Level in a single one hour video. When I informed the Office, they said "no dice." They'd already sold the tapes as two volume sets; so I had to come up with another solution.

The answer was to shoot more tape, but this time with a plan in mind. I made a list of images I needed, particularly sets of bad examples of movements and how to fix them, to be intercut with the material from California. George Williams, who was then at Tempel Farm and later became both the Vice President of USDF and the rider of the elegant mare Rocher, was enlisted to turn my shooting script into visual reality with his students' and his own riding. In addition I sketched 96 simple diagrams that were formalized by an artist and semi-animated to flesh out the explanations of the geometry of various exercises. Then I went into a studio in Ocala, laid down the two hours of narrative, and sent it all back to Nebraska to be assembled.

I'm happy to say that my Smoke and Mirrors Technique did the trick, and that the finished *On the Levels* looked "intentional" and was well received. But this really was a textbook example of how NOT to make a video!

71

Curb Your Enthusiasm
(Three Bears Version)

Some of us assume that a positive, upbeat attitude is a "given." Why would anyone go to all the trouble to do this sport if she didn't love it? Reason Number One: her mother....

I was teaching at the National Pony Club Festival at the Kentucky Horse Park a couple of years ago. The kids came for their lessons in groups of three, and when the first contingent arrived one bright morning, one rider seemed especially dour. As usual I began by asking them what they'd like to work on. This kid had no opinion.

"So why are you here?" I ventured.

"My mother made me sign up."

"And what do you think about dressage?"

"I hate it."

"OK. Well, listen, maybe you can help me then."

She looked mildly curious.

"I usually watch "SportsCenter" first thing in the morning, but I didn't have time 'cause I had to catch the bus out here. But I do have my *USA Today* with me that I got in the hotel. So, here, take the sports section, canter a 20-meter circle, and read me the baseball scores from last night."

Picture her then with the paper spread out across her lap, cantering the circle, reading aloud, "Red Sox 7 Yankees 6; Braves 2 Phillies 1...."

She was amused; I was amused. Dressage lessons weren't so bad after all.

An *over*abundance of enthusiasm can have its downside too, especially if the party in question is your horse....

I was judging the Beginner Novice Rider division of a horse trials up west of Lake Michigan one summer day. The arena was grass, 20 by 40, and made of plastic chain. The rider was a 40-ish gentleman of uncertain skills on a kind, heavy draft cross. We were ensconced in a big SUV parked at C. Horses were warming up in an open field behind me.

It was a hold-your-breath-for-the-rider kind of test. "If he's going to get killed, God, please let it be after he gets out of my ring!" I was thinking, whereupon I caught a glimpse of a moving blur in my side mirror and heard my scribe shriek, "Look out!"

With that, dashing by, within touching distance of my door, came a riderless horse from the warm up, loose reins flapping. The horse leapt the chain, heading approximately down the centerline towards my judg-ee. Followed closely behind, inches off his port quarter, by *another* horse from the warm up, this one *with* his rider, or more precisely, with his passenger.

I had visions of the entire division from the warm up joining them along with my rider and disappearing into the forest in a mad stampede and shouted for him to PLEASE GET OFF. NOW! FAST!

135

The duo swept by him, circled the field once, and settled down to be captured and ushered back to where they belonged. My rider remounted, and his horse finished the test displaying a whole lot more energy and enthusiasm than how he'd begun.

Then there's the kind of enthusiasm that's just right. I have a teenager who's been showing Second and Third level. She, in turn, has a little sister—11 or 12 years old—who doesn't ride but who comes out to watch for a few minutes and brings me a Gatorade or a bottle of water. One day she appeared at ringside with a plate of chocolate cookies for me that she'd made herself.

"Wow, Taylor," I said teasingly, "These are really good, but you know what I really like? Scallops wrapped in bacon."

The following Tuesday I had settled in to teach Big Sister when Taylor popped up again, this time with a plate of scallops wrapped in bacon, each one skewered with a toothpick. Her mother informed me that Taylor had wanted to start preparing them at seven that morning, but she'd been persuaded to delay until much closer to the afternoon lesson.

I was charmed with her efforts and, being on my best behavior, didn't ask her for the remoulade sauce.

72

Tilt, Tilt, Tilt
Any Surprises Here?

Years ago I gave a few after-banquet speeches that I directed to the husbands in the audience and tried to explain dressage to them. One misconception I thought they naively and logically might hold and that I tried to dispel was that there was any such thing in our sport as a level playing field.

I've been told that somewhere there are some car races where by the rules everyone drives exactly the same vehicle, each one set up exactly the same way. Until cloning becomes more commonplace, that just won't happen with horse competitions, and even then, each horse would have to have been raised and trained exactly the same way. An impossibility.

The results of a dressage show don't tell you who the best rider is, nor who the best horse is, nor even which the best trained one is. They do tell you which pair (among those that happened to be entered that day) one person, the judge, (or occasionally a panel of judges) thought earned the most good points movement by movement through the pre-agreed-upon pattern some committee (the members of which each having their assorted axes to grind) invented. That's a little different!

Along these lines I recall trying for years to prevail with an athletic but very hot Thoroughbred I owned. As an event horse Adam was strong, fast, and a little nuts. Those same tendencies manifested themselves in the dressage arena, but we were great pals, and he eventually competed in the FEI classes. On a day to day basis, though, he wasn't the most rewarding horse to show, either spiritually or score-wise. While he and I were coping with each other, another FEI horse fell into our hands. He had a few holes in him but he was a superior mover and was considerably more laid back. Both Susan and I showed him successfully, and when people saw me on him, some remarked about how much better my riding had become. No matter what they thought, I knew that it had taken much better riding to attain the meager goals I'd realized with Adam than the more visible accomplishments I had made with the new horse. But so it goes. That's what I mean by an unlevel playing field about which we shrug our shoulders and just soldier on.

73

Potatoes, Eggs, and Salad

Now first off, I don't want to hear anybody asking "Where's the Beef?" But here, direct from the Dressage Pantry, come three ideas to help you with Acceptance.

When our friend Charlotte Trentelman's new home was being designed, I remember her asking the architect if it *had to* have a kitchen. I know this is the spirit in which many riders approach their more domestic responsibilities; so I'll keep it simple.

Ever made a baked potato in the microwave? Stick it with a fork a few times, pop it in, punch up four minutes, and stand back. Then comes the dressage part—how to get it from the oven to the plate over on the island. If you grasp it firmly in your hand, you end up with a blistered palm. If you don't give it enough help to get to the plate, the potato ends up on the floor. The solution is to more or less juggle it from oven to counter.

In other words you don't "hold" it per se, but you surround it in its journey across the room. That's closely related to the idea of influencing your horse as necessary but keeping him in self-carriage as you ride through the movements.

The "egg" part of the story has to do with a receiving hand. Put down your book for a moment, go to the fridge, and get two raw eggs. (Presumably you store them in their shells.) Take your eggs outside and loft one straight up in the air as high as you can. As it descends at you, brace your arm, stiffen your elbow and open your palm as the egg hits your hand. Most likely the egg will break and splatter. As they say, the yolk will be on you! That's the first half of the demonstration.

Take your second egg and throw it up the very same way. This time as it comes down, soften the reception by lowering your hand almost in time with the egg so as to arrest its descent. That relates to the feeling you need to have in the outside rein if your horse is backed off and you're trying to get him to reach into the contact as you send him forward. If he perceives your hand like the first example, he'll hit the bit when you drive, and he'll retreat from it and hollow. While you have to set meaningful limits with horses, there are many that need a "cushy" enough contact that they aren't afraid to come to it so you can teach them to "give."

The "salad" image is just one of several that relates to a part of acceptance. I could equally well talk about aerating your horse or fluffing him up in front the way you would with a goosedown-filled vest that just came out of the washing machine. But this is the Food Page, so let's do salad.

138

I'm thinking of a made-from-scratch Caesar (consult James Beard if you need more help here). The same way you take that big fat wooden salad spoon and fork and toss the salad before you distribute it to your guests is like the lifting, lightening, expanding way that you make your horse's carriage to keep him from running into himself and locking up. To mix metaphors, self-carriage requires that you produce a soufflé, not a pound cake. He can't be airy if you hold him with strength. He needs freedom to be light.

74

Shameless Commerce Division

Face it, although it has many other rewards, being a riding teacher isn't the most lucrative profession in the world. Some of us augment our income by selling horses, but I'm not cut out for that. Others among us buy stacks of lottery tickets every week and hope or try to entice their friends into investing in some pyramid scheme they've found.

But I've taken my future security and my retirement into my own hands by creating a line of Bill Woods™ training aids and accessories, each designed to answer a pressing need in the dressage community.

You may have noticed how hard it is to teach your horse to stand quiet and immobile, halted at X. To solve this training problem, I offer a short length of garden hose for you to drop from the saddle any time you need a good halt. You know how horses just *love* to stand on the hose, right? Mine comes in two models—green for schooling and clear plastic for actual competition (so the judge won't see it).

My second item speaks to the oft-voiced complaint that riders can sit to the trot just fine without their stirrups, but as soon as they take them back, as they must during a test, they bounce. A careful examination of my rulebook determined that while stirrups are mandatory, there is no mention whatsoever about stirrup *leathers*. My invention allows you to clip your irons directly to your show boots sans leathers and sit as comfortably as if you didn't have stirrups at all. Judges will be too preoccupied with making more important decisions to detect such a minor omission. The set comes complete with an instructional manual that reminds you to remove your irons before going to the concession stand lest you run into the judge or the TD there.

Then there are people who are just too wound up with their horses, their family, and their tests to do a good job keeping saddle pads fresh and tidy. For those riders I present The Chia Saddlepad—it never needs to be washed. You just mow it.

As a judge, I am constantly amazed at how much power and authority some riders assume I wield over them. If it comes from my mouth, it *must* be true. I tested this supposition a few weeks ago at a schooling show. A woman had just finished a test in which she'd made several errors of course. I told her of another product of mine that would help her out, describing a music stand-like contraption that mounts right in front of the withers and holds your test booklet open and readable as you perform. She seemed to be taking this all in; so I went one step further with the tale of a forgetful woman whose husband /optometrist had etched the test protocol on the inside of her contact lenses. When she still nodded agreeably, I escalated to the one about the horse that hated dressage so the doctor fitted *him* with lenses etched with trees and jumps so he always thought he was going cross-country. I don't think she was just being overly polite; I think she believed me.

Meanwhile, not long ago as I finished a schooling session at home, I hung my dirty saddle pad over the stall door and discovered a nearly perfect image of the Blessed Virgin in the sweat mark on its underside. When viewed at just the right angle, it might alternatively have been Elvis. So maybe this is "Good bye." If I don't answer my e-mail anymore, it's because I've heard back from either the Vatican or Graceland, my financial woes are behind me, and my new life has already begun.

75
Follow in Your Books and Repeat after Me
As We Learn Our Next Three Words in Turkish...

On second thought, since I'm trying to get you in a Dressage Way here, let's do German.

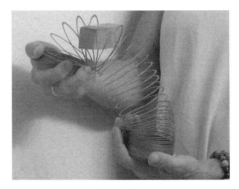

Da!   *Nyet!*

Your Word of the Day is *durchlassigkeit*. A spate of magazine articles some years back introduced everyday American riders to this term along with *lossgalassenheit*, *uberstreichen*, and numerous others. German trainer-authors, in using these terms, were quick to point out condescendingly that English "just doesn't have words to express complicated dressage ideas."

It's an inherent flaw in our language that we can't stick strings of words together to make one long one like they can. Sure they have one word for each idea but it usually has as many letters as the name of some village in Wales!

I've tried adopting this German technique. I refer to one of my former students as, "shewiththebadhandsandenoughmakeuptocoverthecracksinMountRushmore." But I digress.

Durchlassigkeit is related to submission and connection and throughness. Literally "through-lettingness" is a nice made-up synonym. The late Dr. Van Schaik in an article once described it as "permeability." This is a great term. Sometimes when I judge a rigid horse that prevents the rider's half halts from going through, "lacks permeability" just about sums up the problem.

In the same vein, let's talk about "Slinkies." My own thoughts go immediately to one of those little black cocktail dresses but, again, that's getting off the track. Instead, see if you can find one of those metal coiled spring toys from the '50s as in the pictures here. Hold it in both hands, palms up. As you lift your right hand, all the coils pour elastically over into your left one. Reverse which hand is high and which is low and the coils pour back the other way. If you imagine one side is the forehand and one is the hindquarters, you get a nice image of the feel of energy transfer and weight shift that a horse which is *durchlassig* gives you.

In the second photo, the shim of wood is interfering with the flow of energy back and forth. This is what happens when a resistance somewhere in the horse's topline blocks the throughness or permeability I spoke of above.

76

Beyond Connecticut Is a State Where Energy Can Be Stored

I speak, of course, of Potential versus Kinetic energy. If you set the Way Back Machine for junior high school science class, I think we can spot a dressage lesson in here.

People whose riding background is outside the dressage realm obviously have different expectations from their horses than we do. When they decide to have lessons, the first theme we often address is that their horse is A) supposed to notice them and B) care. Shortly thereafter comes the idea that their horse must respond in "real time," not just pretty soon slash when it's convenient.

Sometimes I share with them my experiences of going to yard sales and flea markets. I've been doing this for years always looking to find a real magic lamp. The deal with them is when you rub a magic lamp, the genie is supposed to come out *right away*. If he doesn't, I know it's a defective one and I immediately return the lamp for a refund. That's how promptly and loyally your horse is supposed to respond.

Eventually riders get this part of the relationship percolating, although honestly, with some people it can take them months or even years. At some

point they "get it." And then life gets more complicated. They have to learn to put more energy into the system than they take out.

If you squeeze with your legs and the horse answers by moving forward into trot, he's displaying kinetic energy, the energy of motion. Same thing if he's already trotting and a squeeze or a kick makes him increase his trot. But if you can teach him through greater attention and engagement to "store up" energy for use when you request it, you're creating potential energy. Think of a car battery that holds its charge when the engine is turned off. Or picture a cistern on the barn roof that's filled with water. Simply turn the faucet and the water flows.

When you arrive at this relationship, you no longer have to constantly *make* your horse do things. He's in front of the leg; the energy is stored inside; and when you want to produce a medium trot, your body language *permits* that energy to be tapped and expressed as longer strides. Building the skill to create this Potential Energy without unwelcome side effects like tension or resistance needs to be high on your list if you want to progress into the more advanced levels of dressage.

77
"It's *ALIVE!*"
(From Young Frankenstein)

To continue along with the thread above, having a reservoir of stored energy within your horse is one prerequisite to performing more advanced movements successfully. Another is a useful side effect you garner from the results of a relationship I wrote about earlier in the vending machine story. In that one I spoke of creating a kind of universal preparation where every movement is equally available to you at all times.

Put these two together with the following and the picture comes together: The qualities that you create in one movement cross-pollinate and improve a second movement when you superimpose one upon the other.

Visualize riding a half pass on the diagonal to the left. In this example the half pass will be the overt, visible movement you want to show. Imagine simultaneously riding a less visible undercurrent of left shoulder-in down a line parallel to the original track you left. Those shoulder-in aids keep engaging the horse's inside hind leg, softening his inner jaw, and filling the outside rein, even as they're submerged in the half pass. It is said that the shoulder-in is *alive* within that half pass.

Thinking of complementary pairs of movements reminds you to employ all the relevant aids and not have to invent band-aid, crutch-like substitutes. Colonel Sommer used to counsel, "If you're coming around the corner to make a shoulder-in, prepare your horse as though you want to do Medium on the diagonal." That will ensure that he has the energy and engagement that the shoulder-in requires. He would add, "And if you're preparing for the Medium, have the shoulder-in ready to go." Then your horse will be up and light, and balanced enough to extend.

During every stride of a medium canter, the canter-walk transition should be available. Then the horse won't be running off, dragging you down the track in ballistic flight. If you're executing a turn on the haunches, a prompt walk-trot transition ought to be alive within every step of the turn. In every extension the collection should remain alive. In "very collected canter" the feel of a move-off into big strides should be equally alive.

There are dozens of examples. The point is if the partnered movement isn't alive in the main one, then you need to make it so with interrupting "Excuse me?" exercises that keep your horse thinking and that make those alternatives available.

78

Mind over Métier
"Don't Worry, Boy, Those Dreams Are Only in Your Head" (Bob Dylan)

Dressage, we know, is cerebral as well as physical. The former involves not only mastery of technique but sorting out how to put all your "fears, self doubts, and aching pains of the soul" somewhere that you won't trip over them while you're trying to work.

I was teaching a timid rider on a kind but physically limited horse. The rider didn't lack so much in ability as in confidence. "If only I could get her on another horse so she could feel the right things," I thought, but I doubted she'd ever venture onto something younger or more athletic.

At the time I was also training and showing a 5-year-old Holsteiner gelding who was doing quite well in the All Breeds rankings nationally. I knew this woman would profit from a lesson on him, but how to persuade her?

After much arm-twisting, she agreed to appear at my barn with the proviso that she could back out if she lost her nerve. When I pulled him out of his stall for her, I introduced him, "Pam, this is Buttercup. She's a 19-year-old Quarter Horse, and I think you'll have a good time on her."

She did, indeed, have a nice ride, never worried, and learned some things. Only when we'd finished and she was leaving did I reveal his true identity and resume; but by then the horse as well as her anxieties were back in the barn.

An occasional clinic student of mine had some insecurities about performing but hid them well, seeming not to take anything too seriously. She mainly rode her horse in the low hunters but liked to dabble in dressage, appearing to her friends as a bit of a free spirit.

Hers was the first ride of the day, and a small audience had gathered to watch the lessons. As I greeted her, she leaned down and handed me a short stack of index cards. "Use these," she suggested.

The first card read:

8:10 AM

INSTRUCTOR: This horse has certainly made a lot of progress since the last time I saw him!

The second card:

8:20 AM

INSTRUCTOR: What a lovely pair you are. Very well matched!

The third card:

8:30 AM

INSTRUCTOR: It isn't often that I see a horse this happy in his work!
And so on.

I found my crib sheet worked so well with her that I changed the times on the cards and used them all morning for the rest of the lessons. In fact, I still have them, and it's been six years since she gave them to me. We both learned something that day.

145

79

Fire Away!

A few stories of fire and fireworks both intentional and otherwise:

I climbed out of my car to teach a sometime-student who usually rode a warmblood that she competed PSG. When I arrived, she was on a small Andalusian, explaining that the regular horse had sprung a shoe.

I knew that aside from her competitive endeavors, she traveled the country in the summertime performing at assorted equine expos and conventions. One of her presentations was a group of mini stallions that she used in a liberty act. The Andalusian that I was about to meet was another one.

Did I mind if she had a lesson on him?

"Of course not. What does he do?"

"Well, a little piaffe and passage," she said.

"And have you shown him?"

"Uh huh."

"What level," I inquired.

"Intro."

"Intro?" I puzzled.

"Yes," she explained, "He can't really canter yet."

Given how much he knew about advanced trot work, that answer baffled me.

"Because the stage he performs on is only 40 feet square," she explained. "There's no room on it for him to canter."

As I was adjusting to that information, she added proudly, "But he enters the stage through a wall of pyro!"

So, tell me honestly, can *your* Intro horse do that???

I was conducting an Instructor Workshop for the USDF out in a Deliverance zip code of west central Pennsylvania far from everywhere. I had sent a list of my requirements to them prior to my arrival including a room in which I could show video and moderate a discussion. When I saw the room the first morning of the sessions, it was a little less than I'd hoped for. We were going to have to squeeze ourselves into a very small tackroom and sit on the trunks while I lectured. The room had an un-insulated corrugated tin roof; so when the

146

when the moisture in the air condensed on it, it rained on us in there. I was stoically making the best of things that morning in that cramped space, trying to present my talk. I had set my styrofoam coffee cup on top of the TV to free up my hands, when one too extravagant gesture tipped the cup's contents directly through the slits into the back of the TV. Half a breath later with a loud pop, a flash of fire, and a pathetic eddy of smoke rising from its innards, the set, in one last dramatic Saturday Night Live Moment, expired. The rest of my audio visuals that weekend were confined to shadow puppets.

A student of mine rented a small farm in southwest Florida. The property was owned by a neighbor who let his half-dozen llamas roam in the pasture amid her horses. One evening a group of friends gathered in the back field for a bonfire. Later, when the last toast had been shared and the fire had burned down to a few glowing embers, everybody went home to bed.

Sometime the next morning my student glanced out the kitchen window and noticed one of the llamas was standing out back in a haze of light smoke while placidly munching grass. Upon a second look, the smoke seemed to be coming from him. The llama, it seems, had rolled in the ashes not realizing they were still hot. The thickness of his hair kept him from feeling any discomfort but, yes, he was smoldering.

A well-directed garden hose solved the problem, but the action required certainly lent new meaning to the phrase, "Dear, have you put the animals out yet?"

80
Malfunction Junction

We can always hope that our students follow instructions obediently. Some are just a little better at it than others, and I know that nerves play a big part. I used to teach more event riders than I do these days, and one who was a working student of ours tried very hard but her emotions interfered with her ability to be a thinking competitor.

At one particular event all the dressage arenas were set up in the same 10 acre field, and once the competitors entered that enclosure, they were on their own. Back then the whip rule was different. At a horse trials it could be carried in the warm-up but not in the test itself.

Denise had warmed up smartly for the dressage phase, and her mare looked good. The very last thing I said to her as she left me to circle her competition ring was "Remember, don't forget to drop your whip!"

When the judge's whistle blew, that was the first instruction that left Denise's mind. Thus, by the time she halted at X, whip in hand, she had eliminated herself. Not lacking in creativity, misguided though it was, she proceeded up the centerline, trying discreetly to stuff the dressage whip up inside the sleeve of her black coat so the judge wouldn't notice she still had it.

A three and a half foot dressage whip isn't that easy to camouflage, she discovered. Among other things, it makes it impossible to bend your elbow which is one of those things that even the least involved dressage judge is apt to notice. This judge not only noticed but nearly fell out of her trailer, she was laughing so hard.

Other calamities take place that are beyond our control. Some years ago my wife was conducting a clinic for the Florida Panhandle dressage club that was headquartered on Eglin Air Force Base. This was before we'd made our permanent move south, and I went along to Eglin since we were planning a few beach days after she was done.

Since the Air Force doesn't count riding stables among its highest priorities when it makes land use allocations, the club was located practically at the end of one of the main runways. All day I saw Phantoms and F-15s in afterburner and extraordinarily loud KC-135s passing close overhead of us at the dressage arena. The horses that lived on base hardly noticed them.

Generally speaking, it isn't in my nature to sit idly by during lessons when I could be helping or, at the very least, being a nuisance or getting in the way. Susan, I surmise, put up with this as long as she could and then enlisted our hostess to take me on a trail ride to get me out of her hair for a while.

My guide arrived mounted and ponying their guest horse, a wide-eyed five-gaited thing wearing a western saddle, some kind of curb bit, and moving like an egg beater. I got on and we moved away from the others heading off toward the landing light pylons at the threshold of the runway. My horse hopped across a dry gully and wanted to get strong on the landing side. When I went to check him, the right rein broke right off the bridle! At this point I was out in front of my companion where she couldn't see exactly what was going on, just that I was going faster, swooping around a big circle, and appeared to be hanging on the left rein.

I was having visions of careening down the runway into the air intake of a jet fighter (anything to get mentioned in the *Chronicle*, you know) and hoping the other rein wouldn't break off too. As I sailed past, she shouted, "You can use the other rein!"

"No, I can't!" I shouted back, holding it high in my clenched hand.

When I was able to reel him in and get stopped, I got down and led him back towards the arena. The clinic auditors had watched this whole little episode unfolding and were highly amused by my predicament. A few suggested I was still just seeking attention.

Another time a woman I was teaching caused a car accident and gave me a concussion. She was an impossibly difficult rider to work with—a sweet person but with absolutely no work ethic. She never listened, and she'd frequently and unilaterally stop for "rest breaks" in the middle of whatever I was trying to accomplish. I was sitting in a plastic chair, leaning back against the kickboard in her indoor ring trying to persuade her to make her horse wait for the aids and not just throw in a flying change when he felt like it. I tossed my head back in

Pat Wilker

Susan at Eglin: "Beat the traffic, avoid the tolls, and make those Dead Beat Dads pay up with your F-15 Strike Eagle."

frustration, bouncing it against the plywood. It made such a satisfying echo that I did it again. It didn't hurt, and the noise it made was exponentially more rewarding than the rest of the lesson.

On the plane home that night my head hurt a lot. The next morning I had all the classic signs of a concussion—the dizziness, the nausea—and spent 24 hours flat out in bed. The next day I was still feeling less than 100 percent, but I decided to suck it up and go teach.

Susan said, "Are you sure you're OK?"

"Oh, yeah, I'm fine."

"Well, be careful."

Not careful enough. At the end of one lesson, I jumped in my car, threw it in reverse, and slammed backwards into a large tree that had been there every single week but which I'd forgotten about. The bill was $1500, which I wanted to forward to that woman who'd caused the whole thing, and the insurance agent had the temerity to ask me if the tree was all right.

81
Getting in Step
Sync Before You Sink

A rider who could sit to her horse's trot half way decently was complaining that she couldn't get with him when she tried to go from posting to sitting. He'd always come off the bit.

She demonstrated for me, and the problem was that for that handful of strides, she'd just stop riding altogether. She'd be so busy trying to find the horse's back with her seatbones that the rest of her aids ceased completely.

My advice to her was all about pre-planning and visualization. If you think of a softball team for a minute, when your side is out in the field and your opponents have runners on base, the infielders don't just wait for the ball to get hit and then try to think of something to do with it. Between pitches, they talk it over. "Try to get the lead runner." Or "Let the run score from third and try to get the double play." Before the ball is thrown, they've worked out scenarios of how they'll act in each situation and then they simply put the plan into effect.

Sally Swift encouraged running an imaginary videotape in your head of what was supposed to happen a half dozen strides before it actually did.

If you carry this idea beyond the visual realm so that it includes a mental rehearsal of the kinesthetics and the tactile sensations you're about to experience, the horse's movement won't catch you by surprise.

It's like stepping off a moving sidewalk or onto an escalator at the airport. Your mind sizes up the relative movements and your brain starts walking a little bit before your body has to. Then when you do hit the solid ground or that first different step, you're already in rhythm with it.

In a similar way while you're posting, don't just flop down and hope you meet his back correctly. Visualize the motion your hips need to make for a few steps beforehand. Do the mental kinesthetic rehearsal, and then as you sit and carry out your plan, *keep riding,* giving your horse all the normal inputs he needs to stay correctly on the aids.

82
Taking Your Measure

Horses are smarter than people. If they were doing eHarmony, they'd know who to ditch before the download even finished printing out. I learned years ago how much whatever aura you projected led a horse to decide early on how he was going to treat you.

I used to have school horses 35 years ago when I taught groups of beginners. The riders were supposed to check the roster on the bulletin board to see which horse they were assigned, brush him off, tack him up, and appear in the arena on the hour for their lesson. Usually you could tell by the way a given horse walked across the driveway to the indoor how he would behave for that person under saddle. If Butterscotch had to be dragged into the ring at half a mile an hour like an inanimate object, that did not bode well for the coming hour. If a next-hour rider came to the ring gate and announced "Bristol won't let me in his stall," we were really in trouble.

Early on in my own riding I learned how important it was to learn to bluff. If a horse thought you knew what you were doing, he was much less likely to test you. If your ambiance screamed "Mug me, mug me!" he would often be only too willing to oblige. When I used to ride really nutty horses just a day or two removed from the racetrack, there were times I knew I was being run away with. As long as I didn't let the horse know too, he wouldn't think to take me up on it.

These same mind games go on with sport horses. If they *think* they have you, they do. I run into so many overly self-effacing, tentative riders who blame themselves for everything and are constantly afraid they'll hurt their horse. Ironically, these are the very people who are *least* likely to hurt them. To them I say "Ride like the windshield, not like the bug!" I promise to rescue them if they do something too wrong, but in the meantime, given the conclusions they'll otherwise allow their horses to draw, I'd rather have them do *something*.

83

What's the Word?

Honest, I know all the Forum-approved words. "Lacks engagement." "Needs more self carriage." "Braced through topline."

When we were at Aachen, Major Lindgren jokingly told me that a dressage judge only needs to have four words in his vocabulary: *more, less, slower,* and *faster.*

I find it's more fun to have a few extras. The meaning of some are obvious. Rather than say "strong" or "tight" or "tense" over and over, a word like *incendiary* now and then spices things up and is more descriptive. So too can a ride be too *beige* or *monochromatic* rather than just "lacking expression." A horse that's "diving against the hand" more rightly may be *porpoising*; a horse making an unclear transition from trot to walk may be *dieseling*.

If a horse evades far above the bit into a halt, that can be a *periscope halt*. The explanation for a low score in a canter to walk transition might be *pancaked*. Too massively on the forehand in the down transition and you're looking at a *lawn dart*. A violent and unexplained fussiness can be a *Tourette's moment*.

These sorts of phrases are no fun if you use any of them too frequently, but dredging them out of your storehouse can keep both judge and scribe sharper and give the rider something to think (and perhaps ask) about. A lot of terms aren't rehearsable; they just pop out. *Cypress Gardens Syndrome* refers to a rider who "water skis," letting the horse lean on the hands and pull him around. *CSX* is a freight train, which can apply to a horse in a number of off-balance situations. *Caught the third wire* is a bit more obscure and references the way a jet makes a carrier landing. This would imply that your downward transition was way too abrupt.

If you gig a rider for inaccuracy or wandering, why not offer *Avoid roaming charges*? One rider whose saddle was sliding off to the outside because she hadn't remembered to tighten her girth had to be cautioned *Tipping is prohibited!*

If a horse tries to bulge out of the ring near the gate, there are plenty of boring ways to tell the rider he was resisting. The term *Thwarted escape* at least gives her some credit for presence of mind and managing to avoid an even worse fate.

84

The Coyote in the Coal Mine

I taught a Southern Belle for a time. She was a bit long in the tooth and not very motivated but she loved her horse. Her husband fawned over her constantly, dragging the arena before each ride, holding her water bottle, handing her a hankie whenever she needed to mop her brow.

Her horse, an ex-hunter, also had a number of miles on her. It might be fair to say "she was a bit long in the tooth, not very motivated, but she loved her owner." The Belle usually conspired to have me warm up the mare for her, usually for the first three-quarters of the lesson. She and her husband would sit up in a structure at ringside, which was half shooting stand, half lifeguard stand where they could watch what I did.

One day I brought the horse out into a pristine arena and began to ride some figures in the walk. I turned across from H to M, at M made a quarter turn on the haunches to the right and then a 10-meter half circle back to the centerline. At G I rode a half turn on the haunches and a second half circle. Back at H, I repeated the whole cycle several more times.

I rode down to S and turned towards R. At the second quarter line I rode a half turn on the forehand and kept the medium walk back to S. Repetitions followed.

Then at E, a left turn and straight over to B. Turn on the haunches right and back to E, then a left turn and shoulder-in on the inside track. More repetitions.

Finally, I continued on the track to V and repeated the last exercise several times. Then I stopped in front of the "viewing stand" and said, "So, Rusty, can you tell what I've been doing?"

She puzzled over her answer for a moment and then suggested, "You were using the suppling exercises and the lateral movements to make her lighter and more pliable? So she'll accept the bit better?"

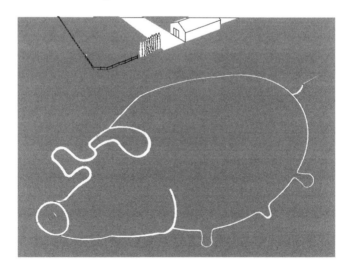

"Well, that's true," I agreed, "But don't you see? I wrote my name!"

I was clinicking one July weekend at a little town in rural Alabama, partaking of the Big Fish Syndrome. My presence was noteworthy enough that the local paper sent a reporter out to cover the visit and the lessons. She was a very pleasant lady who knew little about dressage but, to give her credit, she asked many questions and wrote down every answer.

One question was "Aren't the horses bothered by the heat?"

"Not if we're really careful with them," I explained. "We have the riders carry a big fan to keep them cool, you see. That's the reason they make so many 20-meter circles.... That's how long the cord is."

Just when I was getting rolling (darn!), the organizer pulled her aside and told the reporter that afterwards she'd look over the woman's notes in case anything needed to be amended or modified.

When I judge, I usually use my duck call to signal the next rider in to the ring. It's less militant than a police whistle, less girlie-man than a dinner bell. Once when I was judging at Las Colinas near Dallas I actually accidentally summoned two real ducks to the arena.

Another time I was judging Olympic veteran and USEF President David O'Connor at a horse trials in Georgia. As he finished and saluted at G, he said, "May I speak?"

"Sure," I returned.

"You know, it's really hard," he told me, "to take this dressage very seriously when you keep blowing that kazoo!"

"Please," I answered in mock annoyance, "It's NOT a kazoo." And then pulling one from my briefcase to toot on, "THIS is a kazoo!"

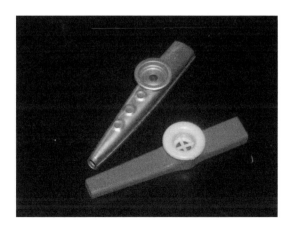

85

Dreidel, Dreidel, Dreidel
(Lovin' That Spin I'm In)

Measure... Proportion... Balance.

Everything about riding dressage comes back to "Enough but not too much." I have a number of students with horses that know more than they do, and the demographics of adult riders put most of those people in the high-functioning over-achiever category. "Effortless effort" is generally foreign to them. I do want them to strive and all that, but I also want them not to get in their own way. They need to find "The Zone."

I teach two women in particular—one from Up North, one from Out West—each with Grand Prix schoolmasters. I introduced them a few years ago in Florida, and they became riding pals and evening wine-tasting co-conspirators.

The next summer I was teaching the Out West one back at her home. We were working on canter pirouettes. During a walk break, performing my "Reach Out and Touch Someone" service, I dialed the Up North student on my cell and handed the phone to Out West as she passed me. They made quick small talk, and as Out West walked by again, I whispered, "Take up the reins and make collected canter."

She did so, reins in one hand, cell to her ear, while narrating to Up North what I was having her do. After a couple of circles I said, "Now at the centerline make a full pirouette."

Up North

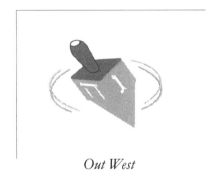

Out West

It worked wonderfully—her horse "sat," stayed soft, kept the rhythm—all the while Out West describing the feeling to her friend as her horse turned.

I haven't arranged it yet, but my Goal in Life is to repeat this exercise with both of them, each in their arenas 2000 miles apart, talking on their cells, and making simultaneous one-handed full pirouettes. I want to capture them both on video so I can create a split screen effect for DVD and show them "in conversation" to my other uptight, overachieving riders.

86

Donkey Rub!

Back in the summer of 1995, my wife and I took two of our Advanced Young Rider students around Europe and to see the Aachen show. We managed to wangle a couple of press passes courtesy of the USDF, and consequently felt duty bound to produce some media-worthy results. We spent the week at the show with Major Lindgren who had been going every year since he'd competed there back in the early '70s.

Anders knew and introduced us to just about everybody. At one point he said to Susan, "So, is there anyone you'd especially like to interview?"

Susan responded that she'd be very happy to have the opportunity to talk to Dr. Klimke. At the time, we were sitting in the competitor's grandstand, and Anders turned in his seat, leaned back, and called over to Klimke in German, "Reiner, would you have some time for my American friends?"

He said he had to find his wife first but agreed to meet with Susan by the warm-up arenas in half an hour. There, she and our working student, Courtney, sat with him and recorded his remarks on a mini cassette player.

When we got back to the States, Courtney's mom, who is an attorney, kindly offered the services of Tina, her secretary, to transcribe the interview. Tina, who knew nothing about horses and even less about dressage terminology spoken with a heavy German accent, produced a fairly amazing document that took us quite a while to decipher. According to her manuscript as delivered, one of Klimke's major concerns was that the horses be "swoo" [rhymes with "shoe"].

157

"Swoo-ness," as Klimke explained, cannot be measured only by the rider's intention. A horse is only "swoo" if the half halts you make GO swoo. Reading the lines in context, we ascertained that Klimke was talking about "throughness" and making the horse "come through" to the bit from behind.

From there we bumbled our way through the rest of the translation until we got to the very end. Klimke had been talking about interactive riding and the need to be willing to experiment with the chemistry between your horse and the aids as one step on the road to discovering what "swoo-ness" really feels like. He emphasized that it isn't realistic to expect instant results, but all good riders have gone through this "searching" stage in their careers many times. There Tina really stumped us.

According to her, Dr. Klimke's concluding words to the American audience were: "Although it may be discouraging at times, "donkey rub!" This mysterious admonition left us both scratching our heads.

"I sure don't remember that!" Susan exclaimed.

But what in the world did he say? My suggestion, "Rosebud," drew a withering look.

We puzzled over all the possibilities to no avail, and frustrated, waited to retrieve the original tape from Courtney's mother. There in a deep voice with his gutteral intonation we heard Dr. Klimke advise his listeners: "Although it may be discouraging at times, DON'T – GIVE – UP." Or as Tina would have had him say, "Donkey Rub!"

Recently I told this story at a Graduate L Judges' Continuing Education Seminar I was conducting. Later through the weekend one participant or another, in the spirit of things, would ask, "That last horse wasn't swoo enough, was he?"

Declared one of the other judges helpfully, "He not only wasn't swoo, he was we-twacted!"

From *Advanced Principles of Dressage and Shellfish, Volume 1:*

RIDE YOUR HORSE

FORWARD

KEEP HIM

STRAIGHT

EAT RAW

CLAMS

My Leg Goes *Where?*

About 35 years ago, before any of us knew what having a horse "on the aids" was all about, someone first showed me leg yielding. "You just put your inside leg behind the girth," she said, "and you push the haunches over." We couldn't do it very well since the horses were, at best, on passive contact, and we had no concept of pushing and receiving aids or the horse being in lateral balance. At the time it didn't mean all that much to me. We had more important fish to fry—like getting to the cross country course.

Then in the fall of '72, I witnessed a rather amazing spectacle. Colonel Nybleaus of Sweden conducted an FEI Judge's Forum at the American Dressage Institute in Saratoga, New York. Nybleaus was a major proponent of leg yielding, while ADI was a bastion of Spanish Riding School emigrees, all firmly planted in the non-leg yielding camp. I remember, as a very humble novice dressage rider, sitting in a lecture room as tweedy, nattily dressed older men with European accents pounded their fists on the table, pointed fingers, and shouted back and forth, "Your ideas will be the death of classical dressage!" "No, yours will!" And so on.

The argument ran: why move your leg behind the girth and teach the horse to move over with him looking back the way he's coming from, when later on, the leg in the same position will be the aid for half pass? Isn't this just a contradiction in training that only confuses the horse?

The next day in the arena I was watching an ADI instructor schooling a young horse. The horse was moving along the track on a shallow angle, forehand to the inside but not bent. "What movement is that?" I asked innocently. "This is shoulder-in," was the reply. "But shouldn't the horse be bent?" I ventured. "Well, of course!" was the answer, "but when we're teaching them, we can't expect them to learn to move sideways and bend at the same time. We do things step by step."

Upon hearing that explanation, I distinctly remember wondering what everybody was so stirred up about the day before.

Several years later, with my eventing career sputtering along and my leg yielding career at a virtual standstill, I had some lessons first with Major Hans Wikne (from Sweden) and later with Colonel Aage Sommer (from Denmark) and Colonel Bengt Ljungquist (then the USET dressage coach and a former Swedish cavalry officer). All three insisted that to execute a leg yielding, one did not bring the inner leg back at all, but rather kept it at the girth.

In subsequent years, as I began to ride with Louise Nathorst (then a young trainer from Sweden working in New England) and with Major Anders Lindgren (from guess where), the explanation became clear:

To the Scandinavians, leg yielding is not just an obedience exercise to teach moving off the leg. It is also a suppling exercise during which the horse is invited to find his lateral balance. In the moment where he is de-stabilized laterally, he can also be re-balanced longitudinally.

Leg yielding is ridden forward to encourage the horse to step up under himself, not just to displace his hips to the side. And, most significantly, it is ridden with almost the same aids as for shoulder-in since it is the center of gravity that is being displaced, not just the hindquarters. The legs are placed the same for both movements—inner leg at the girth and outer leg behind—and only the relative proportions of the aids control whether the horse remains straight, bends a little, or bends as much as a classical shoulder in demands. If the outside shoulder pops and the quarters trail, the inner leg is not drawn back. The advice, instead, is to make a half halt, using the outside rein supported by the forward-driving outer leg (still behind the girth) to make the shoulders "wait" so the quarters can catch up.

I have followed this advice for more than 20 years, using leg yielding, not only for green horses, but to refresh and re-balance more advanced ones in conjunction with other exercises. It just makes sense!

89
Wait, Wait, Don't Tell Me!

Unlike some judges who profess hatred of freestyles, I enjoy judging them. It stands to reason that the more advanced ones are more fun, as are the exotic ones constructed with professional consultation. Still, even a home-made, self-choreographed, and home computer-edited one can look pretty polished these days.

I think the requirement over the past few years that horses must qualify with a minimum 58 percent (or whatever) score at the highest test of their level before being eligible for the freestyle is a good thing. Even with that proviso in place, we encounter too many instances where the judge is whispering something to himself and the scribe like, "Wait! Do you think that's supposed to be a shoulder-in she's riding or is the horse just crooked?" It might seem obvious that to do well, your horse's movements must be recognizable, but maybe that's just me.

Though they're outside the mainstream of competition, sometimes costumed freestyles can be a crowd-pleaser. The best one I ever heard about was done down in Cajun country. The horse was a saintly, well-mannered soul who permitted himself to be surrounded/surmounted by a PVC pipe frame covered with green, purple, and gold bunting. He was a Mardi Gras float, and in keeping with tradition, as his Queen rode him past the bemused judge, she tossed necklaces and trinkets as she would in a real parade.

I've also seen a few quadrilles that were worth the price of admission (had there been one). I judged out in Kansas City a few years ago and the highlight of the whole show was a set of quadrilles put together by a young riding teacher from a local summer camp. She had three groups of four kids, each with jaunty music, and each dressed up in an animal theme with tiger, leopard, or panther wraps, pads, and face paint. And they all could RIDE. What a treat!

A couple of times at Aachen I've watched the German National Quadrille Championships, teams of adults performing freestyle quads at the equivalent of our Third/Fourth Level. Beyond the quality of the rides, to watch the award ceremony's victory lap where six teams of amateurs simultaneously cantered in rank and file in a 20 by 60 arena and weren't even close to annihilating each other was a pretty impressive sight.

90
Changes Are in the Air

A few thoughts about flying changes: Three huge factors in how successfully you'll make them are 1) your timing, 2) the quality of your horse's canter, and 3) how hot your horse is to the aids.

Timing can only really be acquired through practice, preferably on horses that already know the changes and will deliver when you ask correctly. Having said that, watching others do them in person and on tape, counting down to the changes in your mind, and as you watch them be executed, visualizing the body language you'll employ are ways to shorten the learning process.

As for the other factors, you'll run into some horses that appear to have everything they need and yet the changes don't happen. The canter can be fluid, jumping, and expressive, but the horse just won't change.

The key concept you must explore is the nature of the horse's *equilibrium*. To get the flying change, you must be able to shift his center of gravity back, up, and over, and one kind of equilibrium lends itself more to this

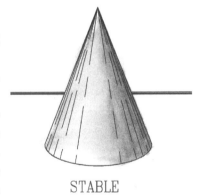

STABLE

UNSTABLE

ability than others. Shown here are examples of two different equilibria. The cone that sits on its wide base is in a stable equilibrium, and only a major effort will upset it. Picture the Training Level school horse that can canter endlessly around the ring on the wrong lead. His momentum and inertia are self-perpetuating, and in his stable equilibrium, he can do this until the bovines RTB.

In the second example, the inverted cone is balanced on its pointed end. If done carefully enough, the cone can remain upright, but this is an unstable equilibrium that can be disrupted relatively easily. Tune your horse's responsiveness to make his equilibrium this adjustable, and your changes have a much greater chance of working!

Another example: here's a very stable airplane, a vintage Piper Cub. There are episodes on record where a pilot flying solo in one of these planes died (of natural causes) while at the controls, and the Cub flew along straight and level until it ran out of gas, whereupon maintaining the same heading, it glided to an unmonitored, intact landing. A plane as steady as this is very unsuited

A husband and his Cub "drop in" for his wife's dressage lesson. I actually took this photo from X.

to performing aerobatics. It just doesn't want to let you change anything that fast.

Its polar opposite is an F-16. It is inherently so unstable that a person can't fly it directly. The pilot uses standard flight controls to tell the plane's computer what he wants the plane to do. Then 40 times a second the computer corrects and updates the plane's control surfaces to make it go where the pilot has indicated. It's so unstable that a person couldn't fly it at all without the computer's help. It is also extremely agile and very good at aerobatic maneuvers.

In other words, the little yellow plane would be terrible at flying changes. The F-16 can do tempis all over the sky. If you want your horse to be able to make good changes, you have to destabilize his equilibrium and make him quick enough to the aids (without tension or loss of rhythm, if you please) to make his center of gravity rapidly displaceable (in real time) both laterally and longitudinally. Then you can *Change* to your heart's content!

91
Begin the Seguin

Day is done. The half halts have been repacked in his Magician's Trunk. The last gratuitous "Brrrav"'s and "Super"'s have been administered. It's time to entertain The Clinician. Bring on the gin and tonics.

Except more appropriate this time were longnecks or three fingers of redeye.

On a rattlesnake freeway outside Seguin, Texas, (and who'd want to be *inside* it, anyway?) sits a cultural icon that may explain why we finally whomped those Rooskies: the Bluebonnet Palace. Picture, if you will, the largest, shabbiest, tin roofed high school cafeteria you could imagine, surrounded by acres of gravel parking lot and more dusty pickup trucks than Davis Monthan has airplane hulks. Inside, the perimeter is lined with a rudimentary bar, usually packed three deep with cowboy wannabes. Their dates (or "the old lady") wait on benches at rows of picnic table style fold-out formica-topped tables. Big

164

hair, big hats, and bling are *de rigeur*. The linoleum "dance floor" is liberally sprinkled with sand, and the band up on stage bangs out successions of tunes that summon couples onto it to skate the Texas Two Step and the Cotton Eyed Joe.

So far, you're saying, "Big Deal." Right? Well, a couple of times an hour, a red strobe up on one wall starts flashing, and the dance floor empties as people crowd into a small connecting shed to watch... *bull riding*. Not some city slicker Fort Worth mechanical bull, either. The arena isn't any larger than half a basketball court, but otherwise it's a rodeo ring. A lot of whooping and hollering follows. One presumes that some money changes hands as well. A few bulls are ridden and then while everybody waits for the ambulance to get back for another load, they all go back to the big room and dance some more.

If visions of the Bluebonnet Palace wouldn't get Mr. Gorbachev to tear down his Wall and hit The Gap at the mall, what in the world could?

92
Oh, Whoa Is Me!

There's an awful lot of moping in dressage these days. Angst. Self-inflicted torment. I see it especially among amateurs. Novice ones are the worst. They in particular seem to take every failed half halt personally, not necessarily hating their horse for his indiscretions but certainly shouldering the blame themselves and brooding, brooding, brooding.

Dressage riders can learn a lot from observers of other sports. A wise old baseball manager cautioned his players that a team (or an individual) is rarely really at its heart as good as it might look when it's on a winning streak. Nor is it really as bad as it looks during a slump. That's why the baseball season is 162 games. It's a long season, and by the end of it, the cream has finally risen to the top.

You need the same kind of attitude when you go out to work your horse every day. Like a ballplayer who needs to stay on an even keel emotionally, you're better off avoiding unbridled euphoria after one good day or paralyzing

www.hetemeel.com

despair after a less successful one. If you owned a small business, you wouldn't jump to some long term conclusion based on a single day's sales. You would learn to take a longer view and look to reach benchmarks at something like six month intervals. That's the way to deal with riding and training issues as well. Self awareness is one thing, but don't imitate the dieter who weighs himself a dozen times a day. There's not any useful information to be gleaned there. Take a breath, admire your horse for what he is, and ask yourself the old political pollster's question: "Are you better off today than you were six months ago?"

And while I'm relaying sage advice, as you look out the window at your horse grazing in his field, don't forget Woody Allen's words: "95 percent of genius is showing up for work each day."

93

Dressage Is Looking Up

I knew a woman in Vermont who taught a lot of teenage girls. Like all dressage riders, they tended to focus on the top of their horses' heads. Suki's solution was to hang pictures of Chippendale-type guys along the skylights at the top of the walls of her indoor ring. Result: the girls spent much more time looking up!

I always threatened to employ a more simple reminder. Have you ever seen those brass nameplates you can order at the tackshop to go on your bridle's crownpiece? Normally they carry an engraving of your horse's name so you grab the right one when you're in a hurry. I proposed giving all my students similar little brass plaques for their bridles that simply warned: "Don't look here!"

And then there's always been my joking admonition to clinic riders with the same down-looking preoccupation: "Look up at the pelican!" or "Look up at the parrot!" I used this line with a rider up on the South Shore of Boston, and much to everybody's shock, there WAS in fact a parrot up in the tree by the arena. A wild one had escaped from somebody somewhere and, without anyone noticing, had found its way to the tree limb by the ring just waiting for my unsuspecting words.

Lastly, Florida weather is always good for a laugh and a reason to look up. Our area is renowned for extremely localized downpours. It's an everyday occurrence during the rainy season to have an inch of rain a mile or two away and absolutely none at your own farm. Most of the time these frog-stranglers move through pretty fast.

However, I was teaching a Miami clinic and had climbed on the student's horse to work out a problem. I was on a 20-meter circle at B and E when the heavens let loose, and—I'm not exaggerating—I rode three or four circles in which every time I crossed the B side of the centerline, I entered a raging downpour, and each time I crossed back over to the E side, it wasn't raining a drop. It was worth looking up just to see if I was imagining things.

94

Doing What Comes Naturally

When I was first teaching years ago, I had brought a teenaged boy along from scratch and he showed some promise. One day the MFH in whose apartment I was living saw us riding out on the road. Afterwards, he scolded me: "He doesn't even know how to turn around!" I was initially offended by the criticism, but upon reflection, I realized I'd been teaching Danny how to equitate but not how to *ride*.

I was teaching very rudimentary, basic stuff in those days, mainly in group lessons on school horses. My students were once-a-week riders—kids in the afternoon, adults at night—who came out the same time every Tuesday at 6, Thursday at 8 (or whenever), and had their lesson with their same group of riding friends each time. Especially with the adults who didn't have a backlog of childhood riding experiences, I discovered it helped if I made them fill in the gaps. After 45 or 50 minutes of semi-technical "Hands down, toes up, stop pulling" instruction, on days when we didn't jump I'd make them play games. At first, the doctors or the social workers or the school teachers had a little trouble getting "out of character," but they soon discovered that riding with the reins in one hand to play tag made them use their bodies, find their balance, and above all, STOP THINKING SO MUCH. Then they could incorporate those feelings into their regular riding.

Some years later I had a big, strong Holsteiner in training. He had a history of taking advantage of his owner, but I was having a pretty good run of success showing him First Level. One day the owner was visiting and Susan was giving her a lesson on him. He was trying his usual routines of tricking her into hanging on the inside rein so he could waft out of the arena, falling over his outside shoulder. About that time I appeared in the ring on an FEI horse I rode. I said to Susan, "May I interrupt?"

Then, with permission, I told her student, "Bernadette, let's play tag. See if you can catch me." I stayed in the walk but by yielding and turning kept eluding her. By and by she got him moving his withers where she wanted and we progressed to the same game in the trot. The punchline is that after five minutes, her horse didn't escape through his shoulder anymore and the circles were round and balanced.

Any way I can build confidence and instinctual riding is helpful.

We had another woman—mid-40s, ex-hunter rider, timid and tentative—who had acquired a very fancy Grand Prix schoolmaster. When she began with us, she was afraid to ride him out of the arena and down to the gate in the driveway. With Susan's guidance she had figured out how to get comfortable and not let him haul her around. One day her lesson was ending as I rode by, and Susan said to me, "Is there anything you'd like to see her do?"

"Yes, let's see her ride bareback!"

This was something that from having learned to ride as an Adult Amateur, she had never done in her entire life. So we took the tack off, popped her back up, and a few minutes later she was sitting to his most delightful, rocking horse collected canter. It was part of the process of discovering to trust herself and her horse.

I'll never forget another occasion. I had taken my group of riders off to a weekend summertime show in Tampa. We'd all had a good day and had gone to dinner together. We might have had a glass of wine or two but not too many. During dinner a quick storm moved through, and we heard the rain beating down hard on the roof. As we came out of the restaurant, the skies had cleared, the temperature had dropped fifteen degrees, and the sunset was spectacular. We all trooped back to the barn to tuck the horses in. We were handgrazing them, standing around enjoying the evening, most of us wearing shorts and sneakers, and someone suggested we should get on them while they ate. A few more leadropes were borrowed and in a leisurely way, standing around morphed into a little trot and canter.

I said to Courtney, our hotshot kid rider who was doing the GP the next morning, "So let me see your tempis."

She smiled and immediately produced one diagonal of nine 2s and another of 15 1s, making it look easy.

It made me feel very happy to have the others see her do that. *That's* the way I want people to be able to relate to their horses and ride!

95

Read My Lips!

Experienced riders occasionally blurt out one of George Carlin's Seven Words in the show ring and are appropriately tsk-tsked and penalized by the judge for Use of Voice. A novice, meanwhile, may blithely chirp and cluck her way through a whole test without even knowing that her vocalizing is costing her points. When I judge, an inadvertent word gets you docked and the test just continues. But if the "minus 2s" are piling up, I usually stop the rider (charging an Error of Course) and remind him or her to try to "keep it zipped."

At a schooling show I warned one woman about Use of Voice, but she was so flustered that as soon as she resumed her test, words again gushed forth. When she halted at G, I suggested that she should learn to ride like an Eskimo. She seemed confused, so I had to tell her the story of the tourist vacationing in Alaska who walks up to an Eskimo fishing through a hole in the ice. The tourist tries to strike up a conversation: "Catching any fish?"

The Eskimo answers, "Mmmmm."

He tries again: "Sure is cold out here."

The same reply: "Mmmmm."

The tourist: "What are you using for bait?"

Again from the Eskimo: "Mmm. Mmmm."

By now the tourist is starting to lose his patience. "OK," he says, "If you don't want to talk, that's fine. I was just trying to be interested."

At that, the Eskimo points to his mouth and through closed lips and clenched teeth, says, "Sorry, I'm keeping the worms warm!"

I've encountered this same rider at a few other shows in the years since then, and she always smiles, points proudly to her mouth, and says to me: "I'm still keeping them warm."

Of course,
there are plenty of times in schooling that it's perfectly appropriate to use your voice. I do find it tedious when a rider delivers a baby talk stream of consciousness narrative to her horse or when the exclamatory "Good Boy!"'s can be heard three farms away. But as Rodney Jenkins, the old jumper rider noted, "The nice thing about a voice aid is that the horse never resists it. It may work or it may not, but they never fight your voice."

When I'm on a nervous horse or one who's being distracted by his surroundings, I often whistle to him quietly. I want his radar tuned to me, and the additional sensory input will sometimes make him think "back over his shoulder" and less about the outside world.

I can think of times when I *want* my students to speak. Some riders get so intense that they almost stop breathing, and I want them to converse with me just to loosen them up. At a Midwest clinic one middle-aged rider was so tense that little electric sparks seemed to be zinging out every pore.

I stopped her and wondered out loud, "Carol, can you sing?"

"Oh, yes," she answered. "I sing in the choir at church every Sunday."

171

"Great," I said, "How about taking up the sitting trot again and sing to me on your 20-meter circle."

She did so and was able to offer up a lilting *Amazing Grace*. I congratulated her both for the song and that she'd begun to breathe again.

Really getting into it, she trotted off again saying, "Listen to this!" She then sang me the same lyrics but this time to the tune of the *Mickey Mouse Club March*. (Go ahead. Try it!)

I told this story at a clinic back East and that time I was rewarded by a rendition of *House of the Rising Sun* sung to the tune of the *Battle Hymn of the Republic*!

96
Be the Decider

Resistance isn't the worst thing in the world. I wouldn't exactly go looking for it, and I certainly don't mean the violent, pulse-raising, Clint Eastwood in *Dirty Harry* confrontational kind. But if your horse doesn't at least mention a contrary viewpoint, you might not be raising the most meaningful questions with him. Charles deKunffy expressed this theme in an article years ago in which he likened horse training to the Hegelian Dialectic. The horse, he said, starts with his Thesis. You, in your riding, present an Antithesis. What emerges, we hope, is behavior modified through persuasion—the Synthesis.

When you meet a resistance, it's hard to know if you're doing something wrong or if you're just running up against that contrary opinion. Commonly, an unsure rider will feel a stiffening in her horse and react by taking the leg off or by giving the rein away. It's a natural reaction. Sometimes in their lessons I have to say to riders, "If you don't have the courage of your convictions, at least have the courage of mine."

You know those detective thrillers that you buy at airport news stands? One recurring plot device in them is the False Bottom to the Drawer or the Hidden Space Behind the Bookcased Wall. When the ruse is uncovered, everything changes. A lot of horses would like to persuade you that the superficial "bottom" they offer you is their total depth. They present a threshold of resistance and hope you either don't notice or back off if they complain when you reach it.

Often right beyond the threshold of that resistance is the softness that comes when the horse says, "OK, I get it. It *IS* easier for both of us *your* way." It isn't just a little better either. Lots of times there's a kind of tipping point, and on the other side, the softness, acceptance, throughness, and understanding are a giant quantum leap better.

You have to be rational. You can't be greedy. You can't demand what your horse isn't prepared to give you. But learn to go beyond (Stage 1) Benign Neglect/ Peaceful Coexistence and beyond (Stage 2) Passive Acceptance to uncover the horse that awaits you. The result is really worth the trouble.

97
Pomp and Strange Circumstances

Back in the early '80s, Tufts University was planning the grand opening of its vet school's state-of-the-art large animal facility in Grafton, Mass. Aside from the ceremony itself, they wanted to create a country fair type atmosphere with lots of horse activities, games, and entertainment on the grounds. My Thoroughbred and ex-eventer, Adam, and I were recruited to be one of the dressage representatives.

We were slated to be one half of a *pas de deux*, but bad weather spoiled the plan, and everything was moved indoors at the last minute. The actual dedication ceremony was the lone exception. It was to be held at the main entrance to the building, and looking for a good photo op, the director of the festivities decided I should ride out through the hospital's front door and "cut" the ribbon with my horse's chest.

On cue, the doors were swung open and Adam was greeted by a startling sight. A contingent of dignitaries had crammed close together all vying to fit in the picture. They were headed by the governor of Massachusetts and the president of the university who were holding a frighteningly short piece of white ribbon between them. Just beyond them stood a half circle of photographers wielding flash attachments and standing beneath bobbing umbrellas in the rain.

173

Mission accomplished!

One further complication: so he could hang his head out his stall door, I had taught Adam over the years to stand placidly behind a leadrope tied across his stall front. He knew it was absolutely verboten to lean on it... and by extrapolation, on any leadrope-like white ribbon held between two politicians.

Adam had no intention of violating that rule or stepping out into the zoo he saw before him. But until he did, the ceremony was on hold. The accompanying photo captures our triumphant moment.

Hidden from view, however, is the desperate Dr. Clarke, who, unwilling to see his plans laid to waste, had his shoulder braced into my horse's rump and was shoving Adam with all his strength out the door and through that ribbon.

98

Making It Better
(to Feed McLuhan's Gaping Maw)

Now understand I like dressage just the way it is. (Well, that might not be entirely true, but let us proceed anyway.) Every time an Olympic year has rolled by, a lot of people bemoan the lack of coverage (and meaningful

174

sponsorship) our sport gets, and they talk wistfully of ways to remedy the situation.

People, it's a no brainer! If we want to play with the big guys, we just have to make dressage more like the sports that *are* popular. Ever been to a hockey game? Periodically a radio-controlled blimp glides above the screaming crowd and drops logo-emblazoned t-shirts to lucky fans. Does dressage have a blimp? Not that I've seen. For that matter, hockey has fights. Every so often, the players drop the gloves and go at it. C'mon, Jessica, why can't we at least do that?

Another possibility would be to merge other sports with dressage. I'm thinking Paint Ball. The sporting world is very into *transparency* these days. What could be more clear to a rider (or more pleasing to the audience) than SPLAT, a large yellow blotch appears on her coat as the judge registers his opinion of the last leg yielding?

More seriously, think of why the networks don't want to cover even big time dressage competitions. It isn't because it's too complicated. Lots of sports are complicated, and commentators manage to gloss over that stuff. It isn't because it's elitist. Even the America's Cup makes it on ESPN2. The problem is that dressage tests *take too long.*

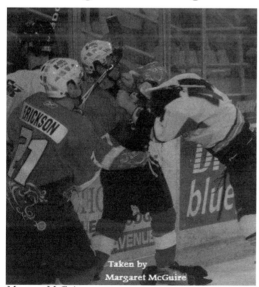

Margaret McGuire

Want to make our sport more accessible and fan-friendly? Place all the Grand Prix competitors in brackets like basketball does for March Madness. Divide the test up into each of its elements. At the beginning of each round, have riders draw to see which movement they'll perform. Line them up in seeded pairs, and have them go head to head, simultaneously riding a single movement—a pirouette, for example. One rider is eliminated; one rider moves on to the next round.

Remember, the post-MTV generation has a short attention span. If it takes longer than six seconds, advertisers will look elsewhere. You may be one of those purists who thinks this would spoil dressage as we know it. But it's up to you. Do you want art or do you want the cash? There probably is no Door Number Three.

99
Silence is Golden

At one point years ago, I was riding in a clinic with German trainer Walter Christensen. Among others, one of his best known students was multiple Olympian from Sweden, Louise Nathorst.

I had taken my Thoroughbred former event horse, Adam, to the clinic. At the time we were working Fourth Level. Christensen spoke a little English but preferred to teach through a translator. During the lesson I was asked to make a canter half pass from F to X and then continue up the centerline toward the gallery. As I approached G, Christensen stood, raised his hand for me to stop, and spoke rapidly (and, to me, incomprehensibly). His translator offered: "He wants to know if you made a half halt to collect your horse before the corner."

This struck me a little as one of those "Have you stopped beating your wife?" questions, but I grimaced and managed, "Well, I thought I did."

Another excited torrent of German followed. The translator: "He says you *did*. It worked! He collected. So why did you keep trying to collect him all during the half pass?"

Once again, I fall back on the words of the Masters—those dressage texts from the 20th century that, in a few words, crystallize important philosophical concepts to hold in your mind. Appropriate to the circumstance described above, it was Mick Jagger who said, "You can't always get what you want... You get what you need." The corollary is: "Give the horse what *he tells you* he needs." The reward both to him and to you after you've made a successful half halt is the subsequent opportunity to do NOTHING. Sometimes the silence can only last a few strides. In more rare but delightful moments, the self-carriage carries on and on. We over-achievers have to be willing to do nothing without feeling we've abdicated some responsibility. A receptive horse is susceptible to stride by stride interventions, but that doesn't mean you necessarily need to be making them. If everything's working, silence can, indeed, be golden.

100

In the Beginning
Dressage Was Without Form and Void

Not all that long ago American dressage was astonishingly primitive. I don't say that critically—it's just a fact. The best weren't very good, and we, the novitiates, were absolutely helpless. I have old 8mm movies we took at major shows and selection trials in the '70s and early '80s. The horse flesh wasn't anything like what we're now used to seeing, even at relatively local shows. Technically, the horses weren't nearly as collected, engaged, or "through" either.

Anna Marie Kirkegaard once related a wonderful tale to me from the early days of the Kennedy administration (circa 1961) of Jackie Kennedy's demand to have dressage classes added to the Washington International Horse Show. Aside from having to schedule them in the wee hours of the night, great questions arose about finding tests, finding a judge (any judge), and over many matters that we just take for granted now.

There were isolated practitioners of dressage scattered around the country but few places where you could go and learn if you didn't have an "in." Into this void stepped a small group spearheaded by Margarita (Migi) Serrell. (I never called her anything but Mrs. Serrell.) If you started your own dressage career sometime after 1980, you probably never heard of her or of the American Dressage Institute, the organization that she founded, supported financially, and of which she was the first president. It began in the mid-1960s as a conclave of like-minded people coming together in the summertime on the Oklahoma Training Track in Saratoga Springs, New York. Spanish Riding School émigrés dominated the teaching ranks. Names you've become familiar with—Hilda

Gurney, Kay Meredith, Linda Zang, and Sandy Howard—were among the students. For a time in the early '70s, ADI had a permanent facility they shared with Skidmore College and a group of remarkable, FEI-experienced school horses that couldn't be found anywhere else in the U.S. In addition, Colonel Hans Handler, then the Director of the Spanish Riding School, brought two Lipizzaners from his program that he donated to ADI at the dedication of the school.

I had the good fortune to be among the smaller group of novice students who attended sessions there in those early days. We were all caught up in an extraordinary atmosphere—fun, yes, but a bit church-like and especially feeling privileged that doors in our minds were opening, doors that up until then we didn't even know existed.

Most magical all those years ago were the evening quadrilles that the advanced riders staged nearby at the Saratoga Performing Arts Center. Concert-goers strolling to summertime outdoor performances of the New York City Ballet and the New York Philharmonic paused to watch *real* dressage on the green lawns outside the amphitheater. To the riders, it wasn't showing off, it was sharing an art they loved.

ADI was a shooting star on the dressage scene too far before its time to be financially viable. Had it been established later, after the USDF and so many local clubs around the country had gained a foothold, it might have continued to flourish. As it was, ADI propelled many of us on our way into a real career in dressage. In recognition of all her efforts, Mrs. Serrell was inducted into the USDF Hall of Fame in 2003.

101
Dressage Supports the Right of a Woman to Choose

Men, too, if you can find any.

Dressage is all about choice, as I explained to an enthusiastic but unfocused new student recently. On one level, it's about choosing which exercises you should be doing with your horse at a given moment during a training session—which ones will help him understand, which ones will strengthen him, which ones have you established enough foundation for in your earlier work?

Then it's also about choosing *how* your horse will perform them. Some horses don't allow you to choose. "Here's my shoulder-in," they seem to be saying. "Take it or leave it."

I've been on "fancy," expensive horses that don't let you choose at all. They're programmed. I tried a "six figure" horse in Germany who made a perfectly credible half pass from M to X. But come a few more meters down the track, counter-position her to yield off the wall, and NO DICE! That simply did not compute. It would be funny if it weren't so pathetic.

In another instance years ago I was the ground person for an eight-member FEI level quadrille exhibition. I was quite amazed to find that while each rider could perform all the movements, they had great difficulty adjusting them to match the strides and speed of the others. This made things a little exciting when they were supposed to "thread the needle" through X making zig zag half passes.

Build into your horse the ability to adjust stride, speed, and carriage, and you won't regret it for a minute. Support a Woman's Right to Choose!

102
Dressage-Bert

I hope your daily non-riding work doesn't confine you to a cubicle like Scott Adams draws in his cartoon strips. If it does, though, you can still learn something about dressage there.

When you first learn to ride, sitting centered, balanced, and unobtrusively out of your horse's way is a primary goal. Some riders learn this lesson so well that they look a little like they're cautiously, defensively balancing on top of a flagpole when they ride.

I remind them that your saddle ought to be your "work station." Put yourself back in that cubicle—real or imagined—and sit yourself down at your desk. Be sure you upgrade to a chair with those little casters on the legs so you can push it around the masonite board on the industrial Berber underfoot. Then you can move around at will. Push off and glide from your keyboard over to the printer. Now to the coffeepot. Now to the fax machine. Now to the waste basket.

That's the same relationship you need to have with your weight in the saddle. The movements are less obvious to be sure, but differing situations call for your weight to be distributed one way or another. I can even think of a few extreme circumstances—take a very unbalanced horse off the track that likes to cross-canter—where I've sat well off center, dumping my hips to the outside with my leg abnormally far back just to teach the horse he could stay on one lead all the way around the arena.

Jennifer Bravick

There's a conventional place you want to sit. Think of it like the "home keys" back when you learned to type, but that doesn't mean your seat shouldn't go somewhere else—as long as you remember to put it back when you're done.

103

P.T.I.

So many remarkably weird things happen to us while we're trying to act like serious, grown-up trainers and teachers.

I was setting up the PA system for a Lindgren clinic at our farm when, Pardon the Interruption, a rider came to me with a complaint: "Excuse me, but there's an alligator by Letter C and he's scaring my horse." Fortunately,

the visitor wasn't all that big, but he did require a lot of wrangling to get a noose over his jaws, maneuver him out of the bushes, and relocate him (surreptitiously) in the neighbor's pond.

At a clinic outside Miami, I was standing on the track watching my student come toward me in shoulder-in. "Pardon the Interruption," I said pointing behind her, "but what's that funnel cloud coming down out of the sky?" It was a true Auntie Em Moment that caused me some major uneasiness until the farrier shouted that I should only worry if it didn't seem to move but kept getting larger. Since the storm was tracking left to right in the distance, I should just go back to my lesson and stop worrying.

Yet another P.T.I.—I was teaching a young woman on a 20-meter circle when I noticed what seemed to be steam coming from under the hood of her car in the parking lot. I tried to ignore it but the "steam" was turning dark and getting thicker. "Does it usually do that?" I asked, pointing. Seconds later, the flames started licking at the wheel wells, and the lesson devolved in swirls of smoke, sirens, and one decidedly distracted student.

A final episode: Once I was teaching in Costa Rica at an outdoor arena that was bounded by a low fence. Beyond the fence the ground fell off precipitously into a deep gulley and a rushing stream. Through the foliage on the opposite side of the gulley I could see a steep hillside pasture studded with large trees and a few grazing cattle. P.T.I.!! A massive white bull suddenly noticed us intruding on his herd and came galloping into view and down the hill. He tried to jam on the brakes as he approached but miscalculated his considerable momentum. From our side of the gulley, we saw him brace all four legs forward, and with an absolutely horrified Ferdinand the Bull, cartoonish-look on his face, skid down the slope on his behind and splash cannonball-like into the stream. He sat there a minute, then picked himself up in as dignified a manner as he could muster, and delicately made his way upstream looking for a place to climb back out, clearly hoping that if *he* pretended nothing had ever happened, we would too.

104

Noodling

In general, I come down very strongly in the camp that supports rigorously accurate arena figures. I want my students to plan each figure fastidiously and carry out the plan scrupulously.

But there are exceptions. Some horses just get a little too smart for *our* own good. We get predictable, and they catch us at it. We may change figures, but you can almost see them saying, "Oh, yeah, now a 20-meter circle *this* way..."

Then it's time to *noodle*. When you do, it doesn't mean you don't have a plan. It just means you disguise it a bit more from your horse than the normal amount of preparation and warning you give him. Every change of direction still gets advance input, but the path you follow over the ground is more unpredictable than usual—think "spaghetti." The arcs vary in length and in the length of the radii that define them.

A little noodling reminds your horse to respond to your weight shifts with an instantaneous, corresponding shift of his own center of gravity. In other words, it tunes him to follow your weight aids.

The precisely organized "randomness" of this exercise will also encourage your horse to wait for direction and think more about you. He won't be able to start guessing and filling in the "let's go here" blanks without being surprised by having guessed wrong.

Don't think you can build a training system around noodling. In most situations on most horses, the classical figures are where they should learn

their lessons of balance, suppleness, and staying attentively on the aids. However, it is a useful, now-and-then option to keep in your bag of tricks to lift a horse out of the "Leave Me Alone, I'm Smarter Than You" doldrums.

105
The Waiting Is the Hardest Part

What's the main reason kids aren't into dressage? It's not so much that it's boring or uncool. It's that everything takes so darn long to accomplish. Try saying to a 10-year-old, "Do the right things and your horse will be much better... in a couple of YEARS." A couple of years is a pretty big proportion of the whole life she's lived so far. Why would she want to buy into that when she can jump around a course of fences day after tomorrow?

There are exceptions but kids don't usually mature enough to do meaningful dressage until they're in the 12-14 year age bracket. Older riders who've been around the block a few more times have it much easier—perhaps not physically, but mentally—because they have developed an appreciation of the concept of Deferred Gratification.

Sure, there are some instantaneous rewards in dressage, but they generally aren't the ones that move young kids to paroxysms of satisfaction and contentment. Our ethos reminds them more of "Drink your milk and you won't get osteoporosis" or "Don't buy gum—Put that money in your college fund."

Deferred Gratification is so central to our sport that I once figured that if I have to cope with it, so should my horse. Here's the routine I taught him: I would slip a sugar cube into his mouth. If he chewed it up, he got a pat on the neck and we went on about our business. If, on the other hand, he

didn't chomp it up but held onto it, I'd give him another. Many repetitions.

Every time he'd wait, he'd get an additional cube. I can proudly report that the record he set was two cheeks full of TWENTY THREE sugar cubes before he had to chew. Some people might think "chipmunk." Others might think "mumps." I think: "*THAT* is a dressage horse!"

106
Barbra's Brother
(Streisand for Dummies)

"If you know you CAN, then you don't need to. If you wonder if you can, then you had better try it." That approach applies to many things in life, not just to dressage. That's why to commemorate my 60th birthday recently I jumped out of an airplane for the first time.

Riding-wise, one of the things you should be able to do is to release your hands forward without anything bad happening. "Anything bad" would include losing the frame, losing the rhythm, losing the bend, or losing the balance. In the Third Level tests you do this in the canter with either one or both hands from quarterline to quarterline on a 20-meter circle. In German it's called *überstreichen*. To avoid the tongue-twisting accent required, I just tell my students to do Barbra's brother, Über.

Even though the tests call for this only in those several specified places, you ought to be able to do it at any time. During a shoulder-in in the trot, during a canter half pass, even during a canter pirouette are some occasions that come to mind. It shouldn't become a rote mannerism, but the ability to make the overt release without ill effect permits you to make less obvious softenings to your horse all the time. If your horse won't let you "give," you can hardly expect him to carry himself.

Barbra's brother ought to be a viable option that always stays alive within your horse whenever he's on the aids. Then you only need to do it when requested by the judge or your teacher to demonstrate to them, to yourself, or to your horse that the release will really work correctly.

Edson Pacheco

107

Round, Round, Get Around
(More for the Spatially Challenged)

"Fingernails on blackboards" for some people, "Leaving the seat up" for others. What drives me crazy (er) are people who can't make decent arena figures. I've been railing about this for years. Circles with corners, circles with flat sides, circles that don't end where they start are just a few examples. Back in the early '80s, Major Lindgren introduced me to using traffic cones in the ring to give my riders aiming points to improve their accuracy. I came back from that year's National Instructors Seminar with his idea and almost immediately found a way to put it into practice.

I lived up on Boston's North Shore at the time, and I used to drive around to teach some of my lessons. As I passed through the little village of Essex, I slowed for road construction, and close by the side of the road I spied an enticingly convenient set of foot-high traffic cones in a neat stack. The workers had gone home. I was alone. My car swung itself around with the passenger's door flush up beside those cones. The door popped open. The cones got in, and after I taught my lesson, came along home with me.

Later that evening I got to thinking. Essex was such a little town. I had probably stolen all the traffic cones their road department owned. And if I read in the paper that one of the stooped little guys who patched their streets had been run over because his work area was unmarked, well, just whose fault would it be? The next morning I got up at dawn before the workers would be back on the job. I put the cones back in my car, retraced my route, and as discreetly as possible set them back on the roadside where I'd found them.

It cost 72 dollars to buy my own set of a dozen cones from a mail order company, but it was worth it to salve my conscience. I used them constantly. At the time, the owner of a pleasant chestnut Quarter Horse was paying me to teach a young man on him. He was an athletic kid without much formal training. In fact, he'd never even *seen* a dressage test, but the woman was desperate to have him show her horse. We worked together through the summer on all the usual themes—rhythm, energy, and acceptance—using the cones to refine his corners, circles, and centerlines. Finally, in the fall the owner entered them in a schooling show. I was quite hopeful about their prospects. He was a shoo-in for a 60 percent, and I wasn't going to be surprised if he did far better.

I had already scheduled another assignment for the show weekend. They'd be on their own, but the prior midweek I gave them one last confidence-building tune up. As I was packing up to depart at the lesson's end and wishing them success, Tommy interrupted me.

"Just let me be sure I've got it right," he said. "In the test, I go *behind* the cones in the corners?"

This was not a development I'd anticipated. "Er, Tom, I've got some bad news for you...." I began. He was a resilient kind of kid, though, and once he got reconciled to the notion that he was *really* on his own without me or the cones, he did just fine.

I had another geometrically-challenged rider who had her lessons on the grass in her backyard. I had marked out an arena for her, but despite that, her approach to circles was novel if not downright eccentric. Nothing seemed to help until one day I saw her husband tinkering in the garage with their riding lawnmower. The solution was simple. I had him jump on it and crank up the engine. Then I directed him to the "arena," put him on a lungeline, and lunged him as he mowed perfect circles for his wife to follow.

While judging in Costa Rica, I encountered another husband's remedy. Standing by the covered arena, I noticed an odd assembly up in the rafters. It was composed of numerous sections of bent ¾" PVC pipe. I said to Lucho, the farm's owner, "Is that some kind of sprinkler system?"

"No, Gretchen has a terrible time with circles," he explained. "I hung some up there for her to follow around under. It keeps her from looking at her horse's neck, too."

I discovered one more way to make my students—some of them, at least—ride better figures: guilt. On my trips out of town to judge or clinic, I often fly out of the Tampa airport. When the wind is from the north on takeoff or from the south on landings, our flight path takes us almost directly over quite a few stables where I teach. My riders' circles improved markedly when I revealed I was checking on their shape from my window seat as I passed above them.

108

Don't Say It If You Don't Mean It
"Attention" Re-re-visited

It was Groucho Marx who said he didn't want to belong to any club that would be willing to admit him. Likewise, while it's nobody's secret that your horse is supposed to be listening to you, an awful lot of people lower their standard in order to make that claim. In the name of "relaxation" I see way too many "flat-liners" and "cheerful vegetables" out there in Dressageland.

So, just what is "paying attention" supposed to mean? Clearly, your horse has to trust you. He can't be worried that your aids will come like thunderbolts with no warning, so you have to build into your horse an intriguing combination of qualities. He must possess mental coolness and confidence yet be physically hot enough to be responsive to light aids.

Here is an image that might help. A lot of nights I get home from lessons, and dinner is on my mind big time. As you probably find in your own life, a bunch of other things usually stand in the way. Check the e-mail; listen to the voice mail; toss the grain in; pick out the stalls. Being the little Dressage Homemaker that I am, I take a solid first step and put a pot of water for pasta on the stove. Then it can heat up while I conduct Phase A of Getting Things In Order. It's ready to boil just as I'm about to head out to the barn, so I cover it and turn the flame down.

When I come back in the house, the water is simmering so close to a boil that I just have to flick the dial back up, and seconds later I can dump the linguine in. That's a pretty close analogy to how your horse ought to feel when he's on the aids—not boiling over but not discouragingly tepid either. Ready on a second's notice to answer The Call.

If you're a (fool)hardy Northerner, you might like this image better. You know better than to let the woodstove go out overnight if you've only got damp kindling left on the porch. You always bank up the coals so that first thing in the morning, you can blow on them, toss in a few logs, and quick as you can, melt that skim of ice that's formed on your toothbrush. While you're riding, your horse's fires shouldn't be allowed to go out either.

If your warmblood is more casual about life than you'd like, you may need to re-think your relationship in light of this picture: I imagine a local woman who conducts her business affairs with a mild, dignified mien. But every Saturday night she slips into her Wynona getup and drives her pickup down to the saloon in West Ocala. She pushes through the swinging double doors, grabs some tenderfoot émigré Yankee bidnessman, and hauls him out into the street. Then she pulls out her six shooters, aims at his feet, fires off a few volleys, and makes him dance. Using your legs and not your gun—that's how your lazy warmblood should be able to react too! If he doesn't, don't forget there's the Hanoverian Heimlich. Wrap those legs around him and pop that chicken bone right out! He'll be way more in front of the leg after you do.

With a lot of horses the thought of a shot of dry gas in the air intake of their "engine" is just what the doctor ordered. Of equal merit is the image I brought home from my first USDF Convention that was held in N'Awlins. Upon registering on arrival, we all received packets with schedules, event tickets, and brochures of weekend happenings.

Each packet also contained a personal size bottle of Tabasco sauce that we were encouraged to apply liberally to anything we ate except the Bananas Foster. I remember Colonel Sommer once observing that dressage without

189

impulsion was only circus. That little squirt of Tabasco—a spicy, heightened awareness—into most exercises you do with your horse will make the result transcend the ordinary to enter the realm of real dressage.

One more idea? I often tell a student that her horse needs to be more *electrified*. Think "sparks." Think "Lit up." But put on your Mr. Wizard hat; there's a bit of eighth grade science hair-splitting to do here. When you "charge him up," don't think of increasing the current. I don't want you to make the horse be more *strong*. What you want to do is increase the voltage—the electromotive force—which energizes the horse and makes him more ABLE. That's what this attention/ energy thing is all about.

109

No Time Like the Right (Amount of) Time

Colonel Sommer used to remind us of this rhyme:

Mind these three
T – T – T
Hear their chime
Things Take Time.

In dressage you don't get extra points for speed. Riders who are in too much of a hurry are inclined to take short cuts. Consequently they don't allow time for the horse's physical strengthening and muscle development. Or they fry his brain.

Having said that, I some-times tell people that teaching your horse to accept the aids and be on the bit is like solving a Rubik's cube. I see a lot of riders who need to pick up the cube and start manipulating its facets. What they seem to do instead

is the equivalent of wandering around the house for the first 45 minutes wondering where they left the cube in the first place.

Over the years I've discovered that riding goals that used to take me a week to accomplish, I can now do in 30 seconds. And other things that I'd try to do in a week are really supposed to take six months. It's the mindless dilly-dallying that I try to discourage.

To these ends I refer my students to a remnant from television's so-called Golden Age, a peculiar game show called "Beat the Clock." On it, married couples were given tasks to perform (usually involving some combination of large plastic balls, bowling pins, custard pies, seltzer bottles, and blindfolds). To win the prize they had to reach the assigned goal a certain number of times in the allotted seconds that were ticking away on a large analog dial while the audience cheered them on.

Some riding chores must be able to be performed with the same sort of alacrity. Example: shortening the reins and bringing the horse from free to medium walk. This kind of evolution isn't supposed to be a complicated procedure that you tiptoe through. Once I know it's feasible, I set the timer for five seconds (or three) and tell them: Beat the Clock! Riders need to hone their skills so procedures are quick, automatic, and reflexive. Putting a time frame on an exercise like this will lead you towards that outcome.

110

Achy Breaky Canter

I was quizzing a Texas woman who complained that her Novice event horse's canter was too fast. "What aids are you using for the depart?" I asked.

Puzzled, she raised an eyebrow at me and answered, "Well, I jest gig 'im 'n go!"

Clearly, this approach bears some refinement. If the first steps of every canter depart are a harrowing adventure for her horse, it's no great surprise that he would harbor some trepidation about whatever might follow.

When I look across the demographic span of riders who make bad canter departs, I lament the demise of the once popular game of Tiddley Winks.

In brief, this involved plinking buttons lying on a baize tabletop into a cup by pressing on their edge with a bigger button (i.e. your "wink"). Whether they landed in the cup or sailed end over end across the room depended on your touch and dexterity. If your canter aids have all the subtlety of Alec Guinness falling on the detonator in *Bridge on the River Kwai*, you ought to expect some fireworks. If you can imagine, having made suitable preparation, your wink calculatingly sliding across the target-wink with *just enough* pressure, then you at least stand a chance for a decent depart.

Here's a different image that might work for you. You can pick up a green twig, bend it abruptly, and it will choose a slightly unpredictable instant to break. That would be like a depart without enough preparation. Alternatively, you can hold it between your hands and with feeling bend it gradually until you feel the fibers of the wood stressing. This is like when you not only take the slack out of the reins but you take the slack out of your horse. Then it takes only one last, refined, succinct twitch and the twig fractures right on cue. Good depart!

With riders who are prone to violent departs, I remind them that while "prompt" is desirable, some advanced tests instruct us to "*Proceed* in Canter." That instruction evokes the picture of a stately royal procession, not a "launching." At the opposite end of the spectrum, tentative riders whose departs are too casual, nondescript, or lacking expression have to be reminded of that British phrase that commands the horse to "*Strike Off* in Canter," an image that denotes the power and engagement that goes with a good depart.

Once you're cantering, life doesn't always get simple which, in itself, is often the cause of many problems. You NEED to simplify it: I see an awful lot of overriding in the canter—people who, while aspiring to be *with* their horses, are inadvertently driving them out of balance, and in the case of more advanced horses, out of collection.

Have in mind that a correct canter should be relatively self-sustaining. The horse may need some occasional input to correct his balance or engagement or suppleness, but you shouldn't have to hold him up, hold him back, hold him in, or bash him forward constantly to maintain the gait. The motion of your hips and back (controlled by your abdominal muscles) should serve primarily to *conduct* the canter rhythm. As you flow with him, think not of your back

and seatbones driving down into him, but imagine your lower legs lifting him up into your seat. Go to Denny's or Cracker Barrel, and check out that claw thing in the lobby where 50 cents lets you manipulate the crane arm to grab the stuffed toy. Think of your canter mechanics as lifting your horse's ribcage and his withers up to you, rather than pushing them down.

Also think of the speed and relaxation of the canter as largely dependent on the horse's longitudinal balance. He can't be either slow or relaxed if he's worried about falling over! Correcting this

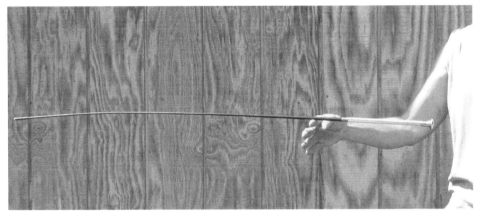

situation requires a series of trials, much like those needed to find the balance point on the whip above.

Your job in the canter: Make your horse shift his weight back with a meaningful half halt. Soften and allow him just a little space to carry himself. As he starts to lose the balance, intervene momentarily, then give him another opportunity to draw the conclusion that he can hold himself up for a few strides. It only takes a few gazillion repetitions. In time, you'll find the horse will suddenly say to you, "Oh, *that's* what you want from me!"

Then your second job is to keep him mentally involved. Refresh him with "pssst" fine touch "I'm still here" reminders—like when you pass by the coke dispenser on the way out of McDonalds and top off that cup *with just another splash* of soda to get you to the car. Work to leave him physically more to his own devices but keep his brain inquisitively devoted to your wishes.

111

Together Wherever We Go

Here's another quick little thought about "connection." Yes, you have to send your horse forward from behind, and, yes, you have to meet him with your hand to give the horse something into which to be pushed in order to gather him. Agreed?

This reminds me of a game we played when I was in elementary school. On rainy days recess was held indoors, and when toys were distributed, the one I coveted most was a set of colored wooden blocks.

One bit of mischief that entertained me was to line the blocks up square to one another on the table and then, while pressing them together uniformly from both ends, to see how many I could lift into the air without the whole kaboodle sproynging apart and flying all over the place. Perhaps the flaw in this analogy is it implies that your horse can be held together forcibly. So in your mind, for the wooden blocks, substitute more fragile foam ones that will collapse and break if too much strength is applied. "Hold" the blocks together by emphasizing their correct alignment and the tactful application of support at both ends and you're closer to the mark.

The twin points that I want to stick in your mind are 1) every "block" must be lined up exactly before you push, and 2) just as you can't collect water in a sieve, if there's no (virtual) cap on the front end, you can't gather the blocks or your horse no matter how hard you push.

112

Bend It Like Bill Would

A bent horse isn't necessarily flexible. Sometimes "bent" is just another word for "crooked." I'll see a horse who appears to be bent correctly, but when I get on him, he feels "stuck"—as though there's grit in his gears or his hinges need to be oiled. A better feeling to look for is a horse who is *pliably adjustable*. The bend he gives you should be available at your pleasure and able to be increased or decreased fluidly and easily.

You can think of an old set of stirrup leathers you've found in the bottom of your tack trunk. They're stiff and almost brittle, but if you clean them up and work conditioner into them gradually, massaging the fibers and carefully increasing the amount they'll bend and twist, in due time they'll get soft again.

Wrenching a stiff horse's neck around roughly will do you no good at all, but it is helpful to teach your horse to soften and give, both in-hand with you standing beside him and at the halt with you mounted.

You'd like him to become so willing to do this that as you slowly maneuver his neck left and

"Oil!!"

right, the weight in the reins is mere ounces. If he won't do it when he's got his weight comfortably distributed on all four legs, you can bet it will be even harder to accomplish in the trot or canter.

What should your bendable horse feel like? If you've ever been to a hockey game, remember how the players move when they come out and warm up before the start of each period. They skate big racetrack patterns, their hips and arms swinging rhythmically like pendulums, everything loose through their whole bodies as they push off with each stride. Or if you've seen a Jacques Cousteau film, picture the way the undersea grasses undulate in the current.

I like to imagine making my horse's neck as pliable as an elephant's trunk. It's not limp and floppy, but unless he's inhaled a crowbar, it's moveable in every direction at every point through its length. When your horse feels like this, then it's no struggle to position him correctly for a half pass or a shoulder-in and you don't need force to keep him there.

While we're on the topic of bending, it's important early on to teach your horse NOT to follow the rein. In other words, if you make him look farther to

196

the right, he shouldn't immediately GO farther to the right.

I found myself once on a horse that did exactly that. I could ride him forward. I could guide him with the inner rein, but that also made him fall through the inside leg as though it didn't exist. I could make no lateral displacement at all towards the outside rein, and as a consequence, it was impossible to make him round.

In this exaggerated case, it was necessary to be heroically strong (we're talking "jackhammer") with the inside leg and reinforce it with the whip on the inside shoulder till the horse reacted.

Cindy West

Once he let me position him right but move his center of gravity to the left, everything fell into place. I could supple him to the inside, and the diagonal aids could perform their gathering function. That one little change in his understanding of the aids that took all of ten minutes to explain to him made all the difference in how he let himself be shaped and subsequently connected and balanced.

113

I Yield to the Distinguished Rider
from the Great States of Premeditation and Order

Tipping. Leaning. Bulging. Wandering in the desert. Oh, you must be leg yielding!

Once you've solved straightening your horse within his own body and his lateral balance, the other question is his alignment relative to the direction he's going and whether he gets to the track where he's supposed to.

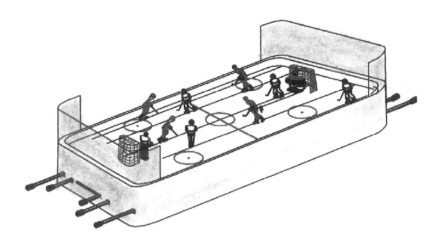

Sometimes I draw a line in the dirt, say from D to B, and calling to mind a San Francisco cable car, I tell my student to imagine a hook extending down from the girth onto the cable under that line. No matter what, keep your horse on that line! If he even begins to deviate behind the line (towards P), send him more forward from your outside leg into your outer rein and up onto the line. If he deviates ahead of it (towards M), your outside rein must make him wait, and the inner leg must push him more to the side.

Then address the question of his alignment relative to the line. A cable car-like image with an additional complexity is the table game shown here.

Each hockey player moves back and forth down his assigned slot on a single line as you push/pull the metal rod in and out. When you twist the rod, the little guy spins, swinging his stick.

The slot is like the line from D to B. As you send your horse down that line, you keep him aligned at a constant angle to it. If he yaws one way or the other, you have to figuratively twist the rod to restore the original angle. If you can make a turn on the forehand, you know how to adjust your horse's haunches relative to his forehand. This is the same coordinated manipulation you make to produce an organized leg yielding. You just make it as a single rotational step when needed, and, oh yes, you do it while your horse is in motion as he continues dutifully down that slot.

Even though the rules call for a leg yielding that's parallel to the centerline with the forehand *slightly* leading, you should, in practice, be able to increase

198

or decrease his angle at your pleasure, even making the haunches lead if you wish.

Then you know you have control of both ends of your horse.

114

It's Ten O'Clock
Do You Know What Yours Hands Are Doing?

People who have trouble maintaining contact with their horses' mouths usually aren't even aware of the problem. I ran across a novel solution to this problem, and it came from a non-dressage rider.

An acquaintance of ours used to ride with Dr. H.L.M. van Schaik on her FEI level Morgan. She was often accompanied by her close friend, George Pratt, who worked at M.I.T. He developed the force plate technology that was able to diagnose lamenesses by the characteristic graphic signature they made when the horse was jogged over his treadles that he tied into a computer. His work was chronicled on a NOVA episode called "A Special Way of Going."

Dr. Pratt, as he audited van Schaik's clinics, noted frequent references to the intermittent contact problem and set about solving it. In his lab he designed a device that would remind you of the kind of spring balance that you might have used in chemistry class. In this case the little scale was to be fastened between the rein and the bit, but instead of a numerical readout, this scale emitted an audible hum that varied as the contact changed. Riders, who would have been otherwise unaware, noticed immediately if the tone warbled up and down instead of staying the same. His gizmo was just for fun and for demonstration purposes—he never intended to market it—but the image of feeling the music of the steady tone through your elbows and triceps is worth recalling when you're trying to learn to ride with consistent contact and a following hand.

On the same subject, I recently encountered a rider who lacked the experience and touch she needed to solve her difficult, defensive Thoroughbred. The horse let her "ride him around," but her contact with his mouth bobbled uncontrollably, and her idea of shaping his topline meant banging him with knife-edge hands which just created more anxiety on his part. I did the usual standing in front of him holding the rein, "You be the horse and feel me follow your motion from my elbow; Now I'll be the horse and you follow me" routine which worked at a standstill, but which she could not carry over to actual riding.

Then I hit on this solution. I got an extra set of reins and tied the original ones up in the mane so she'd have an emergency brake.

Susan Woods

Next I took the new set and fed them through the bit rings without attaching them, the way you would with draw reins. But rather than fasten the bit end to anything, I attached small weights that equaled the amount of contact I wanted her to feel and let them hang free below the horse's jaw. That way, when she used her hands, her rein effects never hit the horse. She felt contact through her elbows with the help of the weights drawing against her, and she felt her horse react more receptively to her hands in a way that she could apply with her conventional reins.

[Note! Before you try this at home, the actual setup is a little more complicated than shown in the picture. As is, if you let go of the reins, the weight will pull all the way through to the ground, which your horse may think is just too weird to deal with. Two additional short pieces of twine which go from the bit ring to the weight will limit how far the weight can drop down. The rest of the time the short strings hang slack.

This may seem like a long way to go for a concept, but if it makes "the light go on," it's worth it.]

Another strategy I haul out from time to time is The Old Yarn Trick, but only in just the right circumstances. Various horses that hang or lean need a strong intervention from their rider to correct the problem. But sometimes they lean simply because the rider's hands inadvertently give them the platform to lean on. Then, as in the example above, I knot up the reins at the withers to be an emergency brake, and I produce a second set of reins. These I hang over the horse's neck, but rather than fasten the rein to the bit conventionally, I hook the end back to itself at the stud making a closed loop. Then I fasten the rein to the bit with a short piece of yarn, smile, step back, and invite my student to ride.

Usually, the yarn will break and the rein will pop off in their hand a few times, but when they get the feel of a still meaningful but lighter relationship with their horse's mouth, he stops hanging and everybody's happier.

There's also a trick that works on people who can't help but pull on the inside rein, overbend their horse, and lose him through the outside shoulder. It happens when they're no longer "aiding" their horse. Instead, they've fallen into a routine that their body performs almost reflexively whether it does any good or not. What is required is that they Get Outside Themselves, and I help them do this by crossing the reins over the withers and putting the left rein in their right hand and vice versa. Again, the invitation: "Now ride."

At first there's a fair amount of accidental weaving and wandering, but then—revelation! Because now when they pull on the inside rein, the horse feels it on the outside, and his shoulder comes into line. And since they've freed his inside jaw (because their outside rein isn't in the habit of pulling on it), he doesn't overbend any more. With a little practice, they can navigate fairly well, and they become more aware of the *effect* the reins are having at their "business end" rather than focusing on what's going on with their hands.

I should mention that before I began doing this to my students, I practiced this exercise on my own horse. I can now ride Second Level Test 4 with the reins reversed in case they call me on it.

Hot Legs
Locked, Cocked, and Ready to Rock

"In front of the leg" means different things to different people. To me, it implies instantaneous response, both forward and sideways. It can't be measured simply by whether the horse is moving forward or by how fast he's going. A horse who's on the aids is "in front of the leg" even in the halt and in the rein back. On the other hand, a pony galloping full tilt cross country may not be in front of the leg at all, a fact that becomes apparent to his rider only when they slide like a reiner into the ditch they've discovered in their path. That pony would be seriously behind the leg. Contrast it with a jumper that can walk to 4'6", and with one squeeze from the leg, take a single trot step, and clear it easily.

I see a lot of lower level riders making walk-trot or halt-trot transitions that would make a senior citizen trying to text message look fast. Without scaring their horse, they have to get him hot to the leg so that he always answers the doorbell as soon as you press it.

When your horse is behind the leg, try not to bash him harder at the moment you want his reaction. Think that your *aids of preparation* must be more authoritative (that's where the bashing comes in). Then your *aids of execution* can be smaller as though they grant him permission to proceed.

Remember, too, that horses don't particularly respond to pressure. Think of how tight the girth is around his belly, and it produces no reaction at all. You can sit on your horse and very gradually increase your leg pressure till you're squeezing with all your might, and he'll ignore you. What a horse reacts to is *changes* in pressure, and he'll respond even better if those changes aren't monotonous, repetitive "poke, relax, poke, relax" squeezes.

Back when Major Lindgren was relatively new to the U.S. and his English was a work in progress (he'd learned much of it from watching American TV in Sweden), I was the organizer for an Instructors Seminar he was conducting. He kept saying to a woman with a vise-like grip, "No, no. You must use your leg like a picking neb."

This didn't elicit much change as you might imagine.

Finally I sidled over to him and whispered, "Anders, that doesn't mean anything. What are you trying to say?"

"A picking neb," he reiterated, making a tapping motion with his extended forefinger. "Like a bird, a woodpecker."

"Ah ha, I get it." Turning to the rider, I translated, "He means 'don't pinch.' Use your leg to regain his attention intermittently like a pecking beak."

So keep your horse interested, keep him hot (in a good way), don't nag, don't, for pity's sake, be boring to him.

One further thought: being in front of the leg also implies being able to connect your horse back to front. You might argue that if he feels *behind your hand*, he's not really in front of the leg. Here we might be getting into Angels Dancing on the Head of a Pin discussions, but don't get bogged down by semantics. If your horse won't reach to the bit or if he won't stretch long and low with an elastic connection, there's usually something missing in his relationship with your pushing aids. He's behind the leg.

116

Excuse Me? Excuse You!
(The Dog Ate My Homework)

I hate being late for appointments. Mussolini's railroad guys would have loved me. When Susan asks me what time I'm likely to get home from teaching on a given day, a sample answer would be "8:24," and I'm rarely off by more than single digits.

I generally expect my students to honor this same convention, but from time to time there are exceptions. I was teaching a weeklong clinic in the moonscape country of southwestern Wyoming, and one of my riders hadn't shown up as her appointed hour grew near.

"I can't imagine what's happened," the organizer sighed. "She's usually very punctual."

Some minutes dragged by until a massive dust cloud on the long dirt road announced the impending (rapid) arrival of a truck and trailer.

The rig ground up beside us and my student launched herself out of the cab apologizing, "I'm sooo sorry, but I was stuck behind a cattle drive!"

Hard to argue with that one.

Some people are just routinely late. In Florida we have an explanation—they just have their clocks set to the Southern Time Zone. A particular teenager I teach and her mom are notorious, and I've learned to take their vagaries into account when I plan my schooling schedule at shows.

One Friday, Child had classes at school and couldn't arrive at the showgrounds until evening. Mother was to bring Horse so that I could work him during the afternoon. After the usual extra hours had slipped by and there was still no sign of Mother or Horse, I called her on her cell. She was still an hour or so away, but she'd explain her tardiness to me when she arrived.

Seems when Mother stepped into the garage in their suburban home to drive the SUV over to the barn, she found a bear in there with it. She panicked, slammed the door, and got on the phone to the Wildlife Management people at her town hall.

"Just shoo it away," they suggested.

"Not bloody likely," she retorted. "Besides, he's eating a bag of dog food."

"Oh, don't let him do that," the bureaucrat responded. "It's bad for him!"

Mother, aka "Hostage," finally roused him out by much banging of pots and pans, and Bear was last seen trundling off into the bushes dragging his bag of kibbles with him.

The originality of this excuse, even had it not been true, was sufficiently meritorious that The Committee (me) granted a Bye for this one too.

Jennifer Bravick

Another time I would have willingly granted an excuse but none was needed. I was teaching on a sun-drenched spring morning at a riding club in Costa Rica. The club was located in the Valley Del Sol to the southwest of San Jose on the highway to the Pacific. The valley runs east-west with two prominent volcanoes on the north side and some smaller, but formidable hillside slopes that jut up to the south. As I taught, I could see activity high on the southern crest.

Though several miles distant, I recognized parachutists filling their colorful rectangular chutes and being lifted off the summit by the breeze. As I taught my lesson, they soared back and forth along the cliff wall catching the updrafts, but gradually getting larger as the distance decreased. I knew the surrounding terrain was fairly built up, especially around the nearby village of Santa Ana. I wondered where they could possibly land.

"There aren't any open flat areas around here that I can recall," I thought. And then: "Except..."

Yes, they got closer and closer, appearing still larger in my purview. And then hooting and shouting, legs bicycling beneath them, they swooped in for their landing right beside my arena. Turns out this was not an unusual occurrence, just not one I'd been warned about. Unlike me, the horses were distinctly unimpressed.

And, now, let *me* make an excuse. When we were videoing the National Symposium down in Scottsdale one year, the members of the film crew were all excellent at their jobs. But, other than the director, the rest of them had no working familiarity with horses. A horse would shy or jump, and the guys would be shocked. "Why'd he do that? What was *that* about?" they'd ask.

And I'd have to explain to them that horses are, well, just different.

"You know about Dark Matter?" I said to them. "Astrophysicists say that 96 percent of the mass in the universe is invisible and undetectable other than by the way the four percent we can see is affected. I'm convinced that horses can see in more dimensions than we do. When they shy, to them it's over perfectly obvious stuff—maybe even a rushing extra-dimensional locomotive careening past their noses"

Be reasonable. Why *wouldn't* they shy?

117

Practicality Makes Perfect (Enough)

An old friend told me she'd taken piano lessons as a child. She'd never gotten very far, she explained, because she was such a perfectionist that if she made any mistake, she felt she had to go back to the beginning and start over. As a consequence, she never finished a piece.

So while perfection is an idealized goal, you don't need to worry your pretty little heads if it remains elusive. Moments of absolute perfection are achievable although not sustainable. Even the best horses in the world aren't scoring strings of 10s, and in case you haven't checked lately, most of us are riding horses with a tad less capability than the Aachen-by-way-of-West-Palm variety.

With this caveat in mind, let me say a few words about schoolmasters. All horses deserve the best of care. All horses need days off and a chance to hack through the fields. They all also need an opportunity to decompress and be loose and swinging through their backs. But if you buy an old FEI level horse on which to learn the movements, don't think you're doing him or yourself a favor by planning to ride him Second Level in a snaffle until he gets 70 percents. It's probably not going to happen. Most likely one of you will die first. Yes, you want him to be as correct as possible. And, no, you don't want to spend your days doing fancy tricks with him inside-out and off the aids. But, hey, this may be your one chance to learn things no other horse will teach you—so get help—but don't be shy.

A few years ago my wife was contacted by a woman whose husband (this being western Florida) ran a traveling circus that wintered nearby. She had a Saddlebred-type schoolmaster who was supposed to do the High School act in their circus, but she was taking lessons from a local professional who told her the horse needed to "go long and low for a year." But, the owner moaned, "My husband says if I don't get him into the ring in two months, he'll feed him to the Great Cats."

Susan, despite her Ivy League-Effete Snob-New England trappings, is enough of a pragmatist to have told her, "So let's put the double bridle on him and fix up 'the three P's'."

I'm happy to report a favorable outcome. The horse learned his tricks and went on to perform under the (not too) Big Top. And in a final irony, the villain of our tale, the husband, looked the wrong way once too often and himself was dispatched by the same Great Cats he'd threatened her horse with. A sad but true story!

On a less dramatic note, I teach a woman with a handsome 22-year-old schoolmaster. She has gained her Bronze Medal scores on him this spring, and the question is: What to do now? My answer to her is that she has demonstrated that low 60s in Third Level are consistently within her grasp. I would much rather see her tackle Fourth Level and risk a few 55 percents as she works things out than go on and on in Third Level trying to bring her scores up a few more points. This is a horse on which she has no particular Year End High Score Award aspirations, and she'll learn a ton more solving the tempis, pirouettes, and counterchange questions than doing the Same Old Same Old. I hope you agree.

118
Se Habla Tico
Vol. 1~ Dressage Showing 'Down Under'

Costa Rican Nationals refer to themselves as "Ticos," a shortened version of *hermanatico*, which means "little brother." That's who I'm writing about, so once you've consulted your *World Atlas*, you're allowed to ask: "Down Under *What*?" "Down under Miami" is about the best I can offer, but humor me.

Back in the mid '90s I was invited to judge in Costa Rica, and it sounded just too exotic to pass up. Since then, I've been back 15 more times, so obviously, the experience agreed with me. That first time was a more like a movie filmed through a mildly warped lens than a regular judging junket. Multiply the standard air travel misadventures manyfold and land me at the airport in San Jose well past midnight, grateful that I got there at all. Then transport me at breakneck speed through darkened streets still teeming with pedestrians in the middle of the night. Cart me up a narrow mountain road with precipitous unguard-railed drop-offs to a Shangri La overlooking the city lights below. Then deposit me in an elegant, high ceilinged A-frame guest house (I being the sole "guest"), and leave me in my too-wound-up-to-sleep state of mind to explore my immediate surroundings.

After checking out the CD collection and the contents of the refrigerator, I laid out my clothes for the next day to unwrinkle themselves and got ready to douse the light. Since there were no invading flying insects, the sliding glass doors onto the balcony were unscreened. I was enjoying the soft breeze wafting in off the mountain when I noticed an extremely large bat observing me from the rafters above my bed.

Now I don't mean to be a sissy, but my first thought was "Just exactly what kind of bat might that be?" My second thought was "Is this *normal?*" I admit to visions of awakening with its teeth clamped on my throat and wondering if they'd find a translator to explain my demise to Susan. I decided I could get through the night safely if I tented the covers and hid beneath them. Then, as I cowered in the dark, I realized that my judging clothes were arrayed directly under the bat's nocturnal perch. Guano City. Not a good first impression to lay on my hosts/employers.

Dawn came soon, and I was escorted a few hundred yards to the show arena. Before I'd accepted the job, I'd inquired about the Prize List. Did Costa Rica have its own tests, for instance? Would they send them to me so I could learn them?

"We use your tests" was the reply. "This show we're doing the Test Threes."

"Excuse me?"

"The Test Threes. Training Three, First Level Three, and Second Level Three if we have any riders for it. Oh, and we'll have Prix St. Georges."

I later discovered that one ride a day per horse wasn't so much to protect the horses from overwork, but to get everything done before the daily Mother of All Thunderstorms moved in around 2 p.m.

Everything about the facility was truly world class. The footing was fantastic. The arena and the embankment above it were ringed with flowering shrubs. The judge's booth was a piece of architectural art with stained tongue and groove boards set in wrought iron. Flags fluttered in the breeze. Recessed speakers beneath the arena letters piped classical music through the air. And the view to my right looked down through the clouds to the valley and the capital city a 1000 meters below us.

208

The show began with four Intro Level tests, none of them especially good. Then while they were being scored, the arena crew came out, re-dragged the ring, and re-rolled the centerline as seriously as if we were at the World Games. It's a local custom that the judge signs the back of every ribbon and presents them to the riders in the arena. Parents, trainer, and everyone else who can walk join the judge and the competitor in the photos that follow. This ritual is repeated for riders Two through Six (had there been that many in the class).

The show then resumed with four nondescript Training Level Test Threes, a brief interlude before the next round of raking, rolling, and picture taking. First Level Three was much the same. The tests weren't the high point, but the ceremonies went on unabated.

PSG drew more entries than any other level, and interestingly, also produced the highest scores and the best riding. By 1 p.m. I had judged a total of 21 rides, signed and pinned on 21 ribbons, and watched the arena be prepared five times. We were done well before the rain and just in time for a sumptuous luncheon. A large lawn tent graced the hillside overlooking the arena, and a chef with an official Michelin star had prepared a sit down meal (don't even *think* of paper plates or plastic forks!) for all the competitors and local dignitaries. Much more formally than we are accustomed to at home, hosts thanked (and toasted) neighbors. Neighbors thanked (and toasted) riders. Riders thanked (and toasted) me. Gifts were exchanged, speeches delivered. And as the rains began, my host said to me, "And we have a massage arranged for you when you're ready."

I've been back numerous times, and I can tell you the size of the shows and the quality of the rides have absolutely skyrocketed. The judge still signs all the ribbons, and the atmosphere remains light and festive. I'll never forget pinning an Intro class where multiple young entrants had been permitted to ride the same horse. Picture three little kids wearing wide smiles riding bareback one behind the next and the next on their one chunky white horse as they paraded in to receive their prizes.

119

Tico Delights
Vol. 2~ Dressage Showing 'Down Under'

As I found myself making longer and more frequent visits to Costa Rica to teach as well as judge (and explaining to people back home that "No, it's not an island in the Caribbean"), an informal contest developed among my students. If I was to be there for five days, each student was assigned to entertain me for a lunch or a dinner. And to my infinite pleasure, they all tried to outdo each other.

For one midday lunch I was taken to a rider's villa overlooking a golf course and treated to a fabulous meal. After lunch I was invited to rest on the upstairs screened porch surrounded by songbirds in the trees. I had removed my dusty boots before lunch and had left them in the foyer. When I went back to retrieve them before my afternoon lessons, wouldn't you know they awaited me buffed and shiny with new polish. (I don't suppose my New York students are taking notes.)

One dinner was clearly the winner, though admittedly this was another case of an unlevel playing field. My student whose turn it was to do the entertaining was the British Ambassador to Central America. She sent the Jaguar to the hotel to bring me to the embassy. As the iron gates rolled open, I acknowledged a prim salute from the guard, and we motored on up the drive to a spotlit portico where the Madame Ambassador greeted me on the front steps. She told much better stories than I, regaling me over drinks and dinner with tales of her years in India working for the Crown. When the servants had cleared the last plates away, we retired to the library for cognac and to listen to her Fleetwood Mac tapes. Even an ambassador has a life, I discovered.

She was borrowing a pleasant, middle-aged, lower level Thoroughbred. The next day during her lesson, her cell phone rang, and she apologized but said she needed to answer it. The next thing I knew, she was crying.

"It's OK," she explained. "I've been riding for 55 years—nearly my entire life—and I've never owned a horse in all that time. I just bought this one!"

Besides Madame Ambassador, I met a second Subject of the Crown on a recent visit. I was judging an informal show at the Club Hipico La Caraña that permitted me to make brief oral comments to the riders as they completed their tests. The first day my scribe was Costa Rican and could easily translate my English to any of the riders or trainers who weren't fluent. (Many have good English skills.) The second day my scribe was a British woman with "go to the grocery store" Spanish proficiency, but not enough vocabulary to translate dressage terms. "Not much Spanish," she apologized, "but I'm good in French."

Consequently, when needed, a translator would bop down from the scorer's booth to do the honors. Mid morning an American woman I'd taught there in past years and who had lived in Costa Rica for the past decade or more came in to ride the St. George. After her final halt and salute, I asked her how her French was. She responded *en francais* with an ease far exceeding mine. I turned to my scribe, wanting to keep her involved, and said, "I'll critique the ride in English and you can relate my remarks to her in French." Why *not*, after all?

I launched into one of those judgely explanations about getting her horse more connected over his topline, riding the changes all the way through to his poll to make them straighter and more expressive, and so on. I gestured to my scribe that she could now "perform."

She shrugged to the rider and carefully pronounced a heartfelt *"Trés bien!"* That was it!

That's why judges should always have a Plan B.

120
Proprioceptively Yours
You Did It Once. What Did It Feel Like?

Kyra Kyrklund in her book, **Dressage with Kyra**, asks, "How can you describe strawberry jam?" As she says, it's that hard to find words to describe the physical manipulations you must learn and the physical sensations you must elicit from your horse to be a good rider. But until everyone has a well tuned FEI schoolmaster on which to learn, we have to try!

If you want to find the feeling of supple wrists that lets you speak to your horse without blocking him, my advice is "Go soft boil an egg!" It's not the cooking that will help you; it's the eating. If you've experienced a hotel breakfast in Europe, you can picture a three-minute-egg served in its shell on one of those golf tee-like pedestals. You whack the top off the shell with your knife and then, using a small teaspoon in a dip-and-rotate motion you eat the egg contents right  out of it. If you're feeling acidophilusly deprived, you can approximate the same wrist motion by eating your Yoplait directly from its narrow-mouthed container. A "Yoplait Wrist" is also a dressage wrist.

It isn't just the Heisenberg Principle (we're talking Quantum Mechanics now) that states that an object's location can be predictably unpredictable and everywhere and no place all at once. That's part of dressage too. Your aids are a little static, and your horse sets up against you? Maybe they need to swarm around him, appearing here and there the way electrons do around a nucleus.

A slightly more mundane version of this idea is the way you play with a puppy on the bed. You tickle his left ribs, and as he squirms around to "bite" you, you're gone. Suddenly you're tickling his ribs on the other side. And then his tail. And then his chin. You're nowhere but you're everywhere. (If you have PETA-type reservations about this sort of cross-species interaction, the same technique works on younger brothers.)

It's almost a cliché in riding : You pull; they pull. You lean back; they lean forward. And yet I see an awful lot of bulldozing horses around the arena —an ill-conceived technique that Susan refers to as "framming them around" where the driving aids are unrelenting, and the horse never gets a chance either to think amidst your constant physical yammering or to find his independent balance.

You can find a nice alternative riding image to the "bulldozing" paradigm in the world of art. It is the technique popularized by Georges-Pierre Seurat

Photo: Bill Woods; Original artwork by G. Seurat

called Pointillism. You can Google the whole complicated explanation if you don't already know it, but for dressage it amounts to the notion that lines only exist as discrete points spaced closely together.* The aids you give and the resultant movements appear as continuities when viewed from afar, but in the intimate realm shared only by you and your horse, each step and each breath should carry its individual request, response, correction, and reward.

Yet another dressage lesson can be gleaned from an examination of the only

US Curling Federation

Olympic sport that combines the skill sets of shuffleboard and housekeeping—namely curling. Visualize the sweepers directing the stone without actually grabbing hold of it, and let that relate to the way your horse should stay on, i.e., *between*, your aids.

Some pages back, I spoke of watching the old "Ed Sullivan Show" on TV. I remember seeing another dressage sort of guy on that show years ago, although he didn't have a horse. He was a juggler who managed, not to keep three or four balls in the air at once, but to simultaneously juggle

213

a chain saw, a chair, and a ping pong ball. Hold onto that thought. That's the state of mind and dexterity you need to cultivate to be a really good dressage rider.

* This is sounding suspiciously like a principle of calculus too, which leads me to raise the question "Why should you never do calculus while you're intoxicated?" The answer: "Because you should never drink and derive!" ...Sorry.

121

What's Their Line?

Over the years I've taught people with all sorts of jobs and backgrounds. .(If I ever taught YOU, of course you were by far much more fascinating than anyone else.) I've taught several former classical ballerinas. I had a jet pilot in Utah. In Albuquerque, I taught a mathematician who, when I asked him to tell me a math joke, promptly responded "The sine of x over N equals 6... Because the 'N's cancel out."

If you don't get it, write it like this:

$$\frac{\sin x}{n} = six$$

Quite the rib-ticklers, those math guys!

In a single one day clinic I had a standup comedienne, a pro beach volleyball player, and an opera singer. Some of these people would stand out in a crowd. Others' "real lives" defy prediction. I had pegged one bib-overalled, slightly marble-mouthed (to my ear) "good ol' boy" from UCLA (that's the Upper Corner of Lower Alabama) for a handyman or maybe a farmer until the local newspaper reporter auditing the clinic greeted him, "Hi, Judge."

I asked one demure, Laura Ashley-wearing, freckle faced Laura Petrie type if she had a job outside the home, and she said, "Yes, I'm a colonel in the National Guard... Artillery."

"Rockets!" she added, smiling at my witless discomfiture.

214

You've probably guessed that my rapier foot-in-mouth style has gotten me in trouble from time to time. The worst ever was when I was teaching a rather stiff rider and tried to loosen her up in the canter by suggesting that she move around on the horse.

"Take the reins in one hand... Reach around and touch his tail... Now pretend you're a cowboy. Lean forward and reach under his neck like you're shooting Indians."

At the time I was standing against the wall of the indoor arena. A woman auditor beside me leaned close to my ear and said quietly, "I'm an Indian."

Mortified, the best I could awkwardly manage was (gulp) "Ohhh, but I, uh, I didn't mean a *real* one." Clearly PC does have a place in the world.

Another student deserves special mention, and she remains an enigma to me to this day. A college professor who was born in the mid 1950s, she professed in a lesson never to have heard of the Rolling Stones. I mean, come on! It's one thing not to like them or maybe not know their music, but this was extreme! My wife's explanation was that the woman was probably a mis-programmed android. She advised me to try to track the woman down at the motel pool on a show weekend and get a glimpse of her in her bathing suit. Everybody knows that androids don't have belly buttons was her reasoning. That would give the masquerade away and confirm Susan's theory for sure.

A fellow I was taken to meet, but had no occasion to teach, was the Duke of Northumberland. I was being hosted by his niece-in-law (should such a title exist) for a clinic near the Scottish border. The Duke's crib was a real, for-real castle. Think Disney's Fantasyland times ten. It sat on 50 thousand acres, much of which he leased out for farming or mining. The castle was 1000 years old, complete with battlements, drawbridge, courtyards, suits of armor. Right out of the *Castles To Go* catalogue or maybe T.H. White. It was furnished with Louis XIV and decorated with tapestries and original Titians and Canelettos.

All this had been "in the family" for most of forever, but the Duke had to work to keep it. His job, my friend explained, was to walk backward at the head of the Queen's royal processions, carrying her scepter.

Not bad work if you can get it.

122
When the Truth Is Found to Be Lies
(I Commit a Dressage Heresy)

There are the Great Pyramids and there are ones that are just pretty good. Personally, I think the Training Pyramid falls into this second group. I'm not about to argue with any part of it because I certainly agree with the validity of all its elements. Who wouldn't? But I do find it to be at the same time both overly simplistic and overly rigid.

I guess I'm irritated that every lecturer who is touting his legitimacy is using it somehow as the topic of his talk if not on his business card and nametag. It's the post modern version of Dressage PC. I would submit to you that three quarters of this book is Training Pyramid-related even though I've scarcely used the term. In a sense it is so all encompassing that it's pretty hard not to at least talk around it if you're talking dressage at all.

One problem I have with the Pyramid is that it implies a linear progression from the base upward to the apex. We've been (rightly) taught since forever that the basic underpinning of dressage is the establishment and enhancement of three pure, rhythmical gaits. Rhythm belongs as the foundation layer. But some less-experienced rider/trainers are inclined to interpret the pyramidal structure as the need to perfect one stage before you can even begin to delve in the next. In real life, however, sometimes a rhythm problem can only be remedied by facing a connection difficulty or by making the horse straighter or by helping him relax. In other words, EVERYTHING IS INTERRELATED. (Duh!)

It's so Teutonic to have a pyramid. On the internet I've found alternative proposals with all sorts of lines and arrows that circle back on themselves and interconnect every part to every other part. What they may lack in clarity, they at least make up for with complex sincerity.

What I propose is shown above opposite.

Learn the Pyramid first and trust that those Germans got it right. Then take all the terms from the Pyramid and sprinkle them throughout my diagram with the proviso that the overlaps and the directions your arrows flow in the bubble will vary from horse to horse and from situation to situation.

The Training Soap Bubble

Remember, just because slaves built the first pyramids doesn't mean you should let yourself be a slave to the new one.

123
Waxing Philosophical

I'd like to claim that "Philosophical" was what I used to call the '65 Corvair I drove as a kid, but as Richard Nixon would say, "That would be a lie!" It is time, however, to lay a few conclusions on you.

To borrow a Tom Wolfe phrase from The **Right Stuff**, the process of training your horse in dressage is one of "expanding his performance envelope." The significant "but" that applies to test pilots and to each of us is: "...without making the wings come off." We're all too familiar with the fried minds of so many would-be FEI level warmbloods that have been foisted off on the American riding public by European "trainers" to ever want to fall into that trap ourselves. Nonetheless, if you're going to get anywhere, you have to learn to tiptoe judiciously near The Edge and to keep pushing that Edge farther and farther out in front of you.

Second, Major Lindgren always repeated this advice to me: The secret to training a horse is to let *the exercises* do it. Your job is two fold: Number 1—pick the right exercise at the right time for the particular horse you're dealing with. Number 2—be sure you and your horse do the chosen exercise correctly. A particular student of mine was once running into the difficulties of fulfilling these two demands. "Brent," I said to him, "you might look at this as a frustration. I think of it as long term employment!"

Speaking of frustrations, as much as I appreciate that gung ho, "never say die," "don't give up the ship" fervor in riders, I am dismayed when I hear people say: "He was so bad today that I just had to keep after him. It took two and a half hours and ..." There may be one horse in thousands that needs to be approached that way, but he is truly the exception. Realistically, there are going to be days when things just don't work. Maybe your job has your nerves jangled. Maybe you're concerned that your kids are home alone spreading peanut butter on the banister. Maybe your horse has a tiny tummy ache. There are reasons to defer to the exigencies of life. It's not always a surrender to postpone the discussion. Many times it's a practical tactical withdrawal. Think of your computer—reboot and try again tomorrow.

Earlier I spoke of priceless personality traits for riders—self awareness and perspective. They keep your ego in check. At the same time, there aren't too many wusses who make it big time (or even small time) in our sport. I can hear Conrad Schumacher's stentorian pronouncement to his audience: "Ladies and gentlemen, you must have ze SKILL and ze VILL." I second the motion.

It all comes down to judgment. You make a thousand decisions every time you ride, but fortunately most all of them are reversible if you discover you've erred.

Back in the early '90s, at the National Instructors Seminar at the University of Nebraska, Eric Lette and I were sitting in the background as Major Lindgren lectured. His talk covered all the varying effects different bits on your double bridle would have on your horse's performance. A set of transparencies projected on the big screen at the front of the hall showed tight and loose curb chains, long and short shanks, thick and thin mouthpieces. Then he put up another slide with different shaped curb bits and asked the group how they would choose which one to use. The room got silent as no one was willing to go out on a limb and venture an answer.

"Ooo, ooo, (Reference 'Officer Gunther Toody') I know. Call on me," I said, springing up.

He looked sideways at me, like "why are you answering?"

"It depends on the weather," I proclaimed.

Silence.

"Because in a storm, any port will do!"

124

Say What?
Famous Last Words

I would have said this stuff myself, but these people were not waylaid by the demands of barn work or the time it took to replace my old incandescent light bulbs with those squiggly Green ones.

I think everybody has heard this quote by now but maybe not in a dressage context—the Albert Einstein definition of insanity: "constant repetition of the same behavior while expecting a different result." This speaks to the need to keep an open mind in your training and not to get so bound up in dogma that you lose any chance to be more creative in exploring solutions.

Here's the flip side. It's from Captain Etienne Beudant, a Frenchman quoted by Jean Saint-Fort Paillard in his own book, **Understanding Equitation**: "If you don't ride the way you believe you should ride, you end up believing that you should ride the way you do." Creativity is part of our art, but what makes it a classical discipline is its foundation in the lessons already learned over the past 400 and some years. What SHOULD be must guide us not only to our goal but along the route we take toward that end.

On the topic of horse training, former USET 3 Day coach Jack LeGoff said: "I can teach a horse to jump off a 12-foot drop into 30 feet of water… (pause) One time." Implicit in this quote is the question "But is that the point?" Everything we do has ramifications, some of them not immediately evident even if you're looking for them. Long term effects, whether they be effects on our horses, on our society, or on our environment, are the epitaph that we write for ourselves. Beyond "in the least to have done no harm," we can hope to influence the nature of humane discourse not only with horses but, by example, among ourselves.

I'm not sure who said this. It was a redneck sportswriter who had probably never heard of dressage; so his remarks were directed at fans of gymnastics, diving, and figure skating, but he could just as well have been ragging on us: "ANYTHING THAT REQUIRES A JUDGE AND NOT JUST A SCOREKEEPER ISN'T A SPORT—IT'S AN OPINION." As much as we try to make our scoring transparent and objective, this objection has a certain ring of truth for which we have to apologize. We do the best we can.

Everybody's hero, Yogi Berra, might have been talking about dressage when he said: "You can observe a lot by watching."

And finally, I met a guy who was married to a dressage rider. He himself was a cop and, after his wife had given him some lessons, became a mounted policeman. I was staying at their home while I was doing a clinic, and over a beer or two, he made the ultimate pronouncement about the value of dressage: "It feels so much better," he said (presumably tongue in cheek), "to have a horse that's soft, and supple, and carrying himself WHEN YOU'RE CLUBBING DEMONSTRATORS."

With this, I must end. Gracie, say goodnight!

Acknowledgments

My profound gratitude to:

The Instigator

I am Mr. Caution. Why jump off the high board if you can dangle your toes in the shallow end first? Wife, Susan, is like the kid who pokes the sleeping bear with a long stick. She did it in 1981 when she MADE me apply to attend the National Instructors Seminar. She did it again when she recognized that what I intended to be a blog on our website could really be something more. This book is the result.

The Liberator

Major Anders Lindgren taught me much about riding and teaching over the years, but especially he helped me realize that neither had to be deadly grim to be productive.

The Enabler

I never thought I'd be this grateful to a math teacher. Mrs. Higbee, who had to suffer my presence through eighth grade geometry, for reasons known only to her, had a shelf full of old **Reader's Digest**s in the back corner of her classroom. Being a "W," my seat was back there next to the bookcase, and when I wasn't cracking jokes with Brad Waldman or trying to peek down Carolyn Werner's frilly bodice, I spent my hours in Geometry reading the **Reader's Digest** anecdotes and falling prey to their beguiling, short, scattershot form.

The Sergeant Major of Word Cops and Phone-a-Friend Reference Diva

Elizabeth Waller, her many skills speak for themselves, among them: her heroic efforts to untangle my syntax. She is said to hum herself to sleep to the tune of "Where Are the Simple Joys of Mavenhood?"

The Chicken

To Chloe Abbatista, the Prairie Rock hen who donated her egg for the cover and whose contribution (unlike dressage) *was* scrambled.

The Reminder

Jill Barrera, *l'etudiante nonpareil*. Many have heard my stories. She apparently listened closely enough to remind me of ones that I'd forgotten but that really deserved to be included in these pages.

The Artist

My Dad, age 89, who graciously agreed to create sketches for those stories I couldn't illustrate with actual photos.

The Editress

Beth Rowland, who gave me a serious run for the title of Most Obsessive-Compulsive.

Special thanks for technical help from Steve Waller, Laurie Vaughn Weisz, and Vindaloo Smith.

And lastly,

The Spiritual Advisor

Jake, the bat-eared French Bulldog, who gets his own story told halfway through this book.

About the Author

Bill's dressage education began at the American Dressage Institute and was nurtured by the Vi Hopkins National Instructors Seminars. He has ridden literally thousands of horses and taught that many more riders at all levels over the past nearly-forty years. For two decades Bill was fortunate to be mentored by Swedish Olympian Major Anders Lindgren.

A USEF dressage judge since 1983, he was also the first American designated by the USDF to conduct official Regional Instructors' Workshops. As chair of the Instructor/Trainer Council, he pushed to fruition the USDF's program for instructor certification and the USDF's program of annual National Symposiums.

Bill was writer, associate producer, and narrator of *The Official USDF Introduction to Dressage* video and for ten years editor of the widely-viewed USDF National Symposium tapes as well as their "voice."

In addition to working with his wife, Susan, from their farm in Ocala, Florida, he travels throughout North America year-round, having judged or conducted clinics in 43 states and five foreign countries.

In 2003, Bill was named at its Thirtieth Annual Convention, as one of the USDF's 20 most influential members in the organization's history.

Readers may reach him thorough his website:
www.woodsdressage.com